A Guide to Non-cash Reward

A Guide to Non-cash Reward

Michael Rose

KoganPage

LONDON PHILADELPHIA NEW DELHI

Publisher's note

Every possible effort has been made to ensure that the information contained in this book is accurate at the time of going to press, and the publishers and authors cannot accept responsibility for any errors or omissions, however caused. No responsibility for loss or damage occasioned to any person acting, or refraining from action, as a result of the material in this publication can be accepted by the editor, the publisher or the author.

First published in Great Britain and the United States in 2011 by Kogan Page Limited

120 Pentonville Road	1518 Walnut Street, Suite 1100	4737/23 Ansari Road
London N1 9JN	Philadelphia PA 19102	Daryaganj
United Kingdom	USA	New Delhi 110002
www.koganpage.com		India

© Michael Rose, 2011

ISBN   978 0 7494 6096 9
E-ISBN   978 0 7494 6097 6

British Library Cataloguing-in-Publication Data

A CIP record for this book is available from the British Library.

Library of Congress Cataloging-in-Publication Data

Rose, Michael, 1953–
    A guide to non-cash reward / Michael Rose.
       p. cm.
    Includes bibliographical references.
    ISBN 978-0-7494-6096-9 – ISBN 978-0-7494-6097-6   1. Incentive awards.
2. Performance awards.   3. Employee motivation.   I. Title.
    HF5549.5.I5R67 2011
    658.3'225–dc22

                                                          2010036666

Typeset by Graphicraft Ltd, Hong Kong
Printed and bound in India by Replika Press Pvt Ltd

For my parents, Felicity and the late Harry Rose

Contents

Acknowledgements xi

About the author xii

Introduction 1

01 Non-cash overview 7

Why non-cash works 7
Conclusion 13
Key jobs to do 13

02 Why recognition is important 15

Introduction 15
Recognition over time 16
Motivation theories 17
Recognition and engagement 22
Recognition in organizations 24
National awards 27
Conclusions 30
Key jobs to do 30

03 What and when should you recognize? 31

What to recognize 31
When to recognize people 39
Key jobs to do 41

04 How should you recognize people? 43

Introduction 43
Who values receiving recognition most? 44
Who should do the recognizing? 47
Recognition as a management practice 48
Peer recognition 53
Customer recognition 53

More formal approaches 54
Cash versus non-cash 57
Creating winners, not losers 62
Key jobs to do 65

05   Designing your recognition programme 67

Defining objectives and successful outcomes 68
What sort of recognition programme? 73
Review what's there 74
Maximizing effectiveness 75
Name of the programme 76
Building a series of programmes over time 76
Using third-party providers 78
Regular review 83
Key jobs to do 84

**06   The cost and effectiveness of recognition
programmes** 85

Measuring the effectiveness of recognition programmes 85
The cost of recognition 90
What should you budget for recognition programmes? 91
Tax and national insurance 93
Key jobs to do 98

**07   How do recognition programmes fit
with HR?** 99

Introduction 99
Recognition and reward 100
Recognition and performance management 102
Recognition and learning and development 104
Role of HR and line management 106
Key jobs to do 107

08   Using non-cash as an incentive 109

Introduction 109
Motivation theories 112
Time span 114
Types of non-cash award 115
Integrated use of non-cash incentives 116

Other non-cash incentives 120
Key jobs to do 121

09 Conclusions and action plan 123

Conclusions 123
Action plan 125
Key jobs to do 126

10 Case studies 127

3 128
BIS 133
Comet Group plc 137
Edexcel 144
Great Ormond Street Hospital 149
Haringey Council 155
KPMG 160
Prudential 167
British Sky Broadcasting Group plc 172
Standard Chartered Bank plc 180

References 185

Index 189

Acknowledgements

I would like to thank the 10 organizations who agreed to feature as case studies, and in particular the individuals in those organizations who were so generous with their time. In addition, individuals within the Ministry of Defence, the Cabinet Office and the Metropolitan Police were very helpful in explaining the public recognition systems they operate.

KPMG LLP not only feature as a case study, but were kind enough to review the tax section of the book. Simply Thank You were particularly helpful in providing information on using a third-party provider. The Gallup Organization were generous with their help and support.

As this book has been developed from one I wrote in 2001, *Recognising Performance,* I would like to thank the CIPD for publishing the first book. I would also like to acknowledge Oxford Brookes University, where I did the original research from which that first book grew and this second book has developed.

About the author

Michael Rose is an independent reward consultant through his company, Rewards Consulting Limited, **www.rewardsconsulting.co.uk**.

Michael's most recent corporate role was Director of Total Rewards for Aon, covering the UK and EMEA. He has also held a number of other corporate HR and reward roles and has a decade's experience as a reward consultant with KPMG and Arthur Andersen.

Michael has an MA in HRM, is a Companion of the CIPD and an Associate of the CII. He was Vice President Reward for the CIPD 2006–8 and was voted Compensation and Benefits Professional of the Year for 2009 by *Employee Benefits* magazine.

Michael writes and speaks extensively on reward and HR issues. His first book, *Recognising Performance*, was published by the CIPD in 2001 and reprinted in 2003.

michael@rewardsconsulting.co.uk

Introduction

Brains, like hearts, go where they are appreciated.

ROBERT MCNAMARA

At the heart of this book are two simple ideas. Organizations should:

- recognize the great things people do; and
- use more non-cash awards to help recognize and incentivize people.

Each of these connected ideas can deliver huge benefits for the organization at little or no additional cost. They are both pretty simple ideas, but if you get it wrong it can cost you more than not doing it in the first place. So this book will help you get it right.

Figure 0.1 gives a definition of recognition and incentives and summarizes their relationship with non-cash.

FIGURE 0.1   Non-cash awards and prizes

Recognition	Incentive
A process of acknowledging or giving special attention to a high level of accomplishment or performance, such as customer care or support to colleagues, which is not dependent on achievement against a given target or objective. It can be day to day, informal or formal.	A material tangible reward that is earned through achieving specific defined aims or objectives that are known in advance.
Recognition is intrinsic reward and is about behaviours and values.	*Incentives are extrinsic reward and are about measures and outputs.*

There are two other definitions that we should get out of the way, as they are used a lot in this book: cash and non-cash:

- Cash is what it says. It may be paid through payroll or it may be a cheque. Tax may be paid by the individual or by the organization. But once the individual has it, they can do whatever they like with it.
- Non-cash is any tangible award or gift that is not cash. It might be small and low in value like a bunch of flowers or a box of chocolates, or substantial and valuable like a flat-screen television or holiday to an exotic location. Non-cash also includes vouchers, which are close to cash but not quite the same.

For many reasons that I explain in the first chapter, I believe it is particularly important to use non-cash to support recognition programmes.

Incentive plans, on the other hand, are predominantly cash based, but can be made more effective by using non-cash as well. A study that offered either cash or non-cash incentives of an equivalent value found that the group who received non-cash awards performed twice as well as the group who received cash. But the cost was the same.

Recognition programmes typically reward behaviours that are linked to the desired organizational culture. They aim to increase employees' motivation and engagement in a sustainable way. Incentives are directly linked to job performance – ie specific outcomes.

Prevalence of recognition programmes

In the USA recognition programmes are much more common than in most other countries. A 2008 World at Work survey found that 89 per cent of organizations had recognition schemes, a slight increase over the data from similar surveys since 2002. While the use of recognition programmes in the UK is some way behind the USA, there has been an increase over recent years, as can be seen from a recent CIPD survey summarized in Table 0.1.

The Chartered Institute of Personnel and Development (CIPD) is Europe's largest HR development professional body, with over 130,000 members in the UK and almost 4,000 international members in over 120 countries. Along with much other research, since 2002 the CIPD has conducted an annual UK reward survey. The 2010 survey had 729 participating UK organizations.

TABLE 0.1 Prevalence of recognition programmes in organizations reporting in the CIPD annual reward survey for 2008–10

	2008 %	2009 %	2010 %
All	36	35	40
By sector			
Manufacturing and production	32	30	39
Private sector services	44	46	41
Voluntary sector	17	15	23
Public services	31	27	59
By size (employee numbers)			
0–49	29	15	27
50–249	28	24	30
250–999	36	35	44
1,000–4,999	47	47	55
5,000+	66	49	72

While there has been an increase overall, by far the largest increase has been in the public sector. It is clear that larger organizations use recognition programmes considerably more than smaller ones.

The 2009 survey produced by Best 600 Companies to Work For – who also produce the annual Sunday Times 100 Best Companies to Work For – ranks companies by one, two and three stars. Of the three-star companies, 51 per cent mentioned some form of recognition in the short notes about them in the Best Companies analysis. No doubt, more use some form of recognition, as only some elements of the employee package are mentioned. But even so, 51 per cent is higher usage in this group of three-star companies compared with the usage reported in the CIPD survey shown in Table 0.1 for companies of similar size. The median size of these three-star companies was 88 employees, so a reasonable comparison might be around 30 per cent in the CIPD survey for companies with 50–249 employees. So use of recognition in these three-star companies may or may not be a contributing cause for their success, but they certainly use recognition more than other similarly sized companies.

It is also interesting to consider the usage of recognition programmes compared with cash-based bonuses and incentive programmes. It appears from Table 0.2 that more smaller companies are using these incentives. In the last year shown, there is little difference in the level of usage between the largest and smallest companies compared with the more marked difference in the use of recognition programmes.

TABLE 0.2 Prevalence of cash-based bonus or incentive plan in organizations reporting in the CIPD annual reward survey for 2008–10

	2008 %	2009 %	2010 %
All	70	70	71
By sector			
Manufacturing and production	84	86	83
Private sector services	88	89	86
Voluntary sector	20	30	25
Public services	34	30	40
By size (employee numbers)			
0–49	56	67	69
50–249	72	66	68
250–999	67	72	73
1,000–4,999	73	78	75
5,000+	77	69	71

The other trend to point out, comparing data in the two tables above, is that although there has been some increase in the use of bonuses and incentives in the voluntary and public sectors, there has been a much greater increase in their use of recognition programmes.

A major UK bank undertook an attitude survey in one of its divisions and found that above all else the most significant cause of motivation problems was a lack of simple day-to-day recognition – acknowledgement or appreciation of what people do. A survey of managers throughout industry found that lack of recognition was cited by two-thirds of respondents as the main factor that would prompt them to hand in their notice. As these two examples suggest, and I will provide more evidence in Chapter 2, a lack of effective recognition, which is common in many organizations, can be an important cause of demotivation and staff turnover. In these highly competitive times, where recruitment and retention are the main concern for many organizations, we need to ensure that we are maximizing our chances of keeping well-motivated and engaged people in our organizations.

This book aims to show how to develop simple non-cash programmes that can have huge impact on motivation and retention at a very low cost. In the following chapters I discuss the range of programmes available and how you can maximize the opportunities and avoid the pitfalls in their design and use.

Chapter summary

Chapter 1 explains why non-cash can be more effective than cash – differentiation, memory value, perceived value and more personal.

Chapter 2 brings many arguments and pieces of evidence together to show the impact of recognition as a driver of employee motivation and engagement.

The first two chapters having given much of the background and evidence of why you should use non-cash awards and recognition, Chapter 3 starts to get into more detail. It covers what sorts of things you should consider recognizing and the most effective frequency for recognition.

Chapter 4 covers day-to-day informal and formal recognition. Within that it discusses the importance of recognition by the manager, of celebrations and non-cash ideas, and how to avoid making winners into losers.

Chapter 5 looks at defining recognition programme objectives and success criteria, using engagement surveys and external providers.

Chapter 6 connects closely with Chapter 5, as it considers how to measure the effectiveness of recognition programmes. It also covers costs, budgeting and tax issues.

Understanding that no programme can make an impact in isolation, Chapter 7 examines the relationship between recognition and reward, performance management, and learning and development.

The bulk of this book is about recognition and using non-cash to support it. But Chapter 8 looks at the use of non-cash reward to support incentive programmes.

Chapter 9 summarizes much of what has been covered in the book and provides an action plan.

The final chapter is the largest in the book. It contains 10 case studies that you should find interesting in themselves. They are from a wide range of organizations and illustrate both similarities and significant differences in their approach to recognition and the use of non-cash awards. I refer to some of the cases by way of example in the other chapters.

Chapter one
Non-cash overview

> *What was the least expected is the more highly esteemed.* **BALTASAR GRACIAN, 1647**

THIS CHAPTER COVERS

- the benefits of using non-cash reward over cash;
- differentiation;
- memory value;
- perceived value;
- more personal.

Why non-cash works

Adrian Furnham, professor of psychology at University College London, believes that non-cash can work well because although people have more choice with money, it doesn't always mean that they get more enjoyment out of how it is spent (*Employee Benefits*, September 2008).

People naturally give a preference for cash rather than a non-cash award. But it does not always mean that because they show such a preference, cash will be as effective as non-cash. This was illustrated by a piece of research undertaken by Scott Jeffrey of the University of Chicago in 2004.

People were invited to a behaviour laboratory to take part in a word game in pursuit of an incentive. They were divided into two groups. One group was given the opportunity to receive cash for high performance in the game. The other group could earn non-cash awards based on their performance. Care was taken to ensure that the value of the non-cash awards was equal to the cash.

In each experiment the non-cash group were asked their level of agreement with the statement, 'I would prefer to receive the cash value of the prize rather than the prize itself.' The result was that 78 per cent said they would rather have the money. However, the groups who received cash improved their performance by 14.6 per cent, but the non-cash groups improved their performance by 38.6 per cent – well over double.

So although the majority of people said, 'I want the money,' using non-cash had more impact on the results. This is an important finding and is a fundamental point underpinning one of the reasons why I believe that non-cash can have a very significant impact over cash. That is not to say that you should do away with cash awards; that would be absurd. You need to pay people a decent salary and give them appropriate benefits. You may also want to have some cash bonus plans. But a tiny percentage of your payroll costs are likely to give you huge value if applied correctly as non-cash awards.

We all like to receive presents; there is something about receiving a tangible award that trumps cash. But there are four main reasons for using non-cash awards over cash: differentiation, memory value, perceived value, and the fact that they are more personal.

Differentiation

Non-cash awards differentiate a recognition programme from pay. Some time ago I was consulting with an organization reviewing their recognition programme. They paid recognition awards through payroll usually a month or more after the event. In one case I found that the period between the event being recognized and the payment was 18 months! Tax was deducted and inevitably the payment was quickly used up in the regular monthly outgoings. Other than a letter informing the individual of the award, there was little or no celebration.

Interviews and focus groups with managers showed that their dominant view was that this was really just part of the pay system; they saw that the important part of the process was the pay. The great majority of recipients, on the other hand, said that the most memorable and important part was receiving the letter of thanks recognizing what they had done. A typical comment was, 'I've worked here for 20 years and this is the first time I've really been thanked.'

Differentiation can be explained by the psychological process of separability, which simply says that people will typically separate different sources and uses of funds and aggregate others (Jeffrey, 2003). For example, most people will mentally separate the appreciation in value of their home from their salary. On the other hand, as both salary and any cash award are earned as part of their job, these are likely to be mentally combined. A cash award lacks separability so that cash that is given, for example to recognize some particular achievement, does not stand out in the mind of the recipient. Although this can be countered by the organization using some celebratory ceremony, it is better to distinguish something outside the norm by using non-cash.

Some organizations I have worked with who use cash awards within their recognition scheme have reported that some of their managers appear to have used these cash awards in 2009 and 2010 to simply top up a very low pay award. If you have a system that allows a reasonably substantial cash award within one process – in this case a recognition programme – it is inevitable that some people will work backwards to find ways to use the money available, where they may be restricted from spending a similar amount within the pay review. Much better is to use non-cash within the recognition scheme and allow some non-consolidated cash bonus within the pay review system. These two are then separate and can be differentiated in the minds of both the managers and the recipients.

Memory value

Non-cash awards can have memory value: that is, their effect is longer lasting than cash. This is also known as 'trophy value'. It is sometimes said that cash is a motivator for as long as it lasts before it is spent. A US survey reported in *Workspan*, November 2006 asked people how they spent their last cash reward, incentive or bonus. The results are shown in Table 1.1

TABLE 1.1   What do employees buy with cash awards?

	%
Bills	29
Don't remember	18
Never received	15
Family gift	11
Household items	11
Savings	11
Special treat	9
Vacation	5
Something else	2

These results hardly support the use of cash if you want some longer-term value. Cash does not bring back fond memories.

In contrast, every time a non-cash item is used or enjoyed, the recipient may remember why and how they earned it. So every time the TV is watched, the individual will be reminded of the organization and their achievement that led them to receive it. Although someone is unlikely to show their neighbour their payslip, it is rather more acceptable to show off something tangible that has been earned. So you would not say to your neighbour, 'I just received an £800 ($1,200) bonus,' but you might proudly show them the new TV you were given by your organization or tell them about the exotic holiday you received. An important component of recognition is the social reinforcement from others knowing about your good performance. A non-cash award is more effective than cash at enhancing this reinforcement as the award will normally be visible, so others will know about it and may well comment or ask about it.

Perceived value

The perceived value of a non-cash award can be much higher than the actual cost, so that a non-cash award is valued more highly than cash of the same value. It may be that the organization can source an award much more cheaply than the individual could. This may be because they are buying in bulk or can negotiate a better deal with a supplier or through a third party. It may be because they can use their own product or services (or those of an associated company) as an award. An example would be a hotel chain providing a weekend stay for an employee and partner or a restaurant group giving dinner for the recipient and family.

The psychological process here is called 'evaluability' (Jeffrey, 2003). That is, a recipient evaluates the award in different ways. When a pleasurable non-cash award is used, people tend to see the positive elements rather than any negative. This is known as an affective reaction to the award or incentive. Jeffrey gives the example of an award of a trip to Hawaii, where the thoughts about the trip will be about lying on the beach with a drink rather than the possible negative aspects such as having to stop the newspapers, taking the dog to the kennels, going to the bank to get currency, etc. This then leads people to use their feelings when determining the value of the award or incentive. This can increase the perceived value of a non-cash award compared with the value of cash which, of course, is easy to evaluate.

A second process that is working here is known as 'justifiability'. In this context it means that even if someone could afford to buy the non-cash gift, they may well not feel that they wanted to spend the money on a luxury or aspirational item that they might think of as frivolous. However, if a non-cash award was viewed as a luxury that the participant valued, but could not justify purchasing, then the individual could justify to themselves its acquisition if it was earned for a particular achievement or hard work.

More personal

A non-cash award can be tailored to the needs and interests of the recipient, showing a greater amount of thought than a simple cash sum would reflect. We only need to think about the difference between receiving a birthday present of a cheque or a really well-chosen gift.

John Timpson, chairman of the UK shoe-repair chain bearing his name, talks about the importance of knowing your people. How can you expect to engage and motivate them if you do not know much, if anything, about them? It is about recognizing the whole person who comes to work. Timpson has put forward the following test, shown as Table 1.2, to challenge managers as to how much they know about their team. He suggests that if you score less than 70 you do not know your people well enough.

TABLE 1.2   How well do you know the members of your team?

Do you know their:	Points
age?	5
address?	5
partner's name?	10
children's name/ages/schools?	20
last holiday?	10
next holiday?	5
main hobbies?	10
partner's hobbies?	5
career history?	10
skills and diplomas?	5
health record?	5
make of car?	5
parents' names?	5

If as a manager you know your people, you can ensure that a non-cash award or gift is personal and will be appreciated. It shows that you know and care about them and have paid attention to their interests and desires. You may be able to find something that they can share with their family or partner. This can be particularly valued where the individual has had to put themselves out at the cost of their partner or family. But it equally holds that if you get it wrong, it can make what should be a very positive event very negative.

Conclusion

We can see that there are some very good reasons to use non-cash over cash. Non-cash can be used as a differentiator; it has memory value; it usually has higher perceived value; and it can be more personal. In Chapter 5 I give some examples of the sorts of things that can be used. Although non-cash can be used in many ways, the two that I think are most common and on which I concentrate in this book are:

- recognition;
- incentives.

As explained in the introduction, they are different, but the arguments put forward here are equally applicable to the use of non-cash for either.

KEY JOBS TO DO

- Consider where non-cash could be introduced.
- Build knowing your people into management development programmes.

Chapter two
Why recognition is important

"There is more hunger for love and appreciation in this world than for bread. MOTHER TERESA

THIS CHAPTER COVERS

- the key motivation theories that relate to recognition;
- the need to emphasize the positive, not the negative;
- recognition as a core element of employee engagement;
- research evidence on the importance of recognition;
- macro-level recognition through national awards;
- learning from the world of education.

Introduction

I define recognition as 'a process of acknowledging or giving special attention to a high level of accomplishment or performance, such as customer care or support to colleagues, which is not dependent on achievement against a given target or objective. It can be day to day, informal or formal.'

That definition looks at recognition within an organizational context. Of course, we could also look at a wider definition that might better get to the essence of recognition as a basic human need: 'The demonstration by human beings that they have noticed and appreciated the actions, achievements and contribution of others. It is fundamental to humans being at ease with themselves, because it is thus that our very purpose is characterized, worthy or unworthy' (Pitts, 1995).

As Curt Lewin's famous maxim goes, 'There's nothing so practical as a good theory.'

In this chapter I present some important research and theories on recognition and its role in motivating and engaging people. I also give some practical examples of where it has been seen to have impact within organizations. This chapter also lays the groundwork for some critical considerations of how you design programmes that I will draw together later in the book. Together, I believe that these give a convincing argument for the importance of recognition.

Recognition over time

The recognition of the great things people do is a fundamental driver that has been understood for a very long time; from at least the early 16th century. Niccolò Machiavelli (1469–1527) understood the need for recognition. He wrote in *The Prince*, 'A prince should also show his esteem for talent, actively encouraging able men, and honouring those who excel in their profession.'

Andrew Carnegie was born in 1835 and was one of the richest people ever. He earned a fortune equivalent to over $300 billion (£200 billion) in 2008 terms from the steel industry. One reason for his phenomenal success was attributed to Carnegie's view of the need to emphasize the positive and praise his colleagues both publicly and privately. He even wanted to do so on his tombstone. He wrote his own epitaph: 'Here lies one who knew how to get around him men who were cleverer than himself.'

In his 1936 book, *How to Win Friends and Influence People* (1936), Dale Carnegie – probably unrelated to Andrew – emphasized that the single most important factor in dealing with people was to recognize the desire to be important. However, he was clear in differentiating between appreciation and flattery – the difference being sincerity. Carnegie said that flattery seldom works with discerning people because it is 'shallow, selfish and insincere'.

Motivation theories

Introduction

While this book aims to be a practical guide, it is nevertheless very instructive to review some relevant theories and research related to motivation in general and recognition and associated drivers in particular. By way of introduction it is useful to mention two aspects of motivation:

- Intrinsic motivation: this is the internal satisfaction in doing the work. 'Behaviours which a person engages in to feel competent and self-determining' (Deci, 1975).
- Extrinsic motivation: this is behaviour resulting from factors external to the individual, such as reward and punishment.

Both are important and the balance between them needs to be considered carefully within organizations. There is a huge amount of research and literature relating to these aspects, which you may wish to explore further, as this is not the focus of this book. But it is a distinction worth bearing in mind and is discussed further in Chapter 8.

Herzberg

Herzberg is probably the best-known motivational theorist. A number of his research conclusions are frequently quoted – or more often misquoted. Even though his research is well over 50 years old, it has some extremely important things to say that can help us design effective recognition programmes.

Herzberg's research among accountants and engineers in the 1950s asked the subjects to recall examples of situations where they had positive and negative feelings about the job (Herzberg, Mausner and Snyderman, 1959). Based on the responses, Herzberg's theory is that there are:

- Motivators that can change behaviour positively relating to job *content* – achievement, recognition (which could come from almost anyone: supervisor, client, peer, etc), work itself, responsibility and advancement.

- 'Hygiene factors', which act as dissatisfiers, relating to job *context* – company policy and administration, supervision, salary, interpersonal relations and working conditions. Although these are commonly the main source of dissatisfaction, they do not become a source of motivation if 'reversed'.

Achievement was the most frequent factor related to positive feelings about the job, followed by recognition. Lack of recognition for work done was a very significant factor for negative feelings about the job. It was also most often the only factor present in the situation, compared with others that more commonly appeared in combination. The research found that whereas achievement on its own can be a source of good feelings about the job, recognition is rarely independent of achievement. 'A feeling that you have achieved and a feeling that you have been recognized are the two most frequent feelings that are associated with an increase in job satisfaction' (Herzberg, Mausner and Snyderman, 1959). Herzberg concludes that the act of recognition, which is not related to a specific sense of achievement, becomes a fairly trivial factor. This finding is a core consideration when we are designing recognition programmes. It is valueless to develop a programme that does not encourage recognition of real achievement.

Herzberg found that the single most important factor that determines feeling bad about the job is company policy and administration. This often appeared in combination with lack of recognition, suggesting that where there was a lack of recognition it might relate to the company policy or administration. Herzberg believed that recognition of individual achievement is unlikely to flourish in a bureaucratic situation. The framework of rules and regulations may constrain the opportunity to display individual achievement as well as the opportunity to recognize it. Again, this is a very interesting finding that should inform our approach to recognition. The strong inference here is that you can damage the potential positive motivational value of recognition by bureaucratizing it. It certainly suggests that very great care needs to be taken before implementing a centralized corporate recognition programme.

Maslow

Maslow (1970) saw motivation in terms of a hierarchy of needs, moving from basic physiological and safety needs through the need for belonging and love to the need for esteem and ultimately self-actualization. It is only when a lower-order need has been satisfied that a need higher up the hierarchy may become a cause of motivation. Maslow's hierarchy of needs is shown in Figure 2.1.

FIGURE 2.1 Maslow's hierarchy of needs

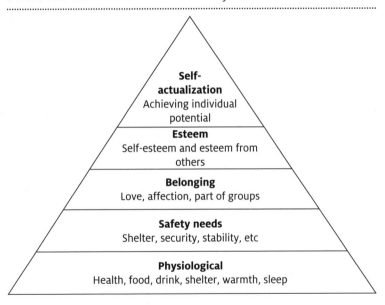

Maslow's 'esteem' need is of particular interest; it is essentially a combination of two elements:

● self-respect or self-esteem, which he sees as 'the desire for strength, for achievement, for adequacy, for mastery and competence, for confidence in the face of the world and for independence and freedom';

- the esteem (or recognition) of others: 'what we may call the desire for reputation or prestige (defining it as respect or esteem from other people), status, fame and glory, dominance, recognition, attention, importance, dignity or appreciation'.

Clearly, recognition needs are linked with the esteem needs in Maslow's hierarchy: improved self-esteem can result from personal recognition from others. This combination of self-esteem and esteem through others is a vital element in the motivational model and one hit squarely by effective recognition.

Social reinforcement

Skinner (1953) developed the model of 'operant conditioning' from work on animals. He found that an animal that received positive reinforcement by being rewarded by food as a consequence of its voluntary action (for example, nudging a lever) tended to repeat the behaviour. Skinner's work followed that of Pavlov, Thorndike and Watson, all of whom contributed to behaviourism. Although this research was conducted using animals, further work has shown that people too will tend to repeat behaviours and actions if they are positively reinforced. Much learning theory is based on this principle.

Stajkovic and Luthans (1997) applied behaviourism within organizations over 30 years and found that there were three types of positive reinforcers that result in an increase of desired work-related behaviours and performance outcomes when made contingent:

- money;
- performance feedback;
- social recognition.

A particularly important finding for us is that 'in many cases feedback and/or recognition, which typically involve no direct cost, often result in similar (and sometimes higher) performance outcomes than monetary reinforcers that are often outside a manager's direct control'. They found that 'Effective social recognition must include personal one-to-one attention and appreciation from the manager communicating to the employee that the desired behaviour has been noticed and admired by the manager versus a standard program where randomly selected employees are recognized regardless of demonstration of desired behaviours (which is what many of the formal recognition programs become over time).'

It is interesting to see how widely recognition as reinforcement is advocated in other areas. In the following example from the world of education, the approach being presented may apply equally to management (Yeomans and Arnold, 2006):

> In order to ensure that desirable behaviour is repeated, it should always be followed by a positive consequence. Therefore, rewarding pupils is an important part of teaching behaviour change. Effective rewards can be things that you say or do. You do not always have to give concrete objects. If you think back to the earlier scenarios, teacher attention to the right behaviour would have resulted in a change. Praise is something that you can give at any time and it doesn't cost anything. Some pupils will do anything for teacher attention, so if that is the case, use it. Doing jobs or having short amounts of individual time with the teacher can be effective. Sometimes just a smile or gesture in the direction of the pupil is enough to tell them that you have noticed their good behaviour.

Negative emphasis

Two more interesting findings come from the world of education. The first examined where focus is put: on the negative or the positive (Rath and Clifton, 2004). A Gallup poll asked the following question: 'Your child shows you the following grades: English – A; Social Studies – A; Biology – C; Algebra – F. Which grade deserves the most attention from you?' The findings are shown in Table 2.1.

TABLE 2.1 'Which grade deserves the most attention from you?'

Country	Focused on As %	Focused on Fs %
UK	22	52
Japan	18	43
China	8	56
France	7	87
US	7	77
Canada	6	83

As we can see, although there were some national differences, in each case considerably more parents would focus on the poor rather than the good results. But, rather than focus on the negative, why not at least start with recognizing and acknowledging the positive before considering what can be done about the poorer results? This sort of behaviour is found in work all the time. As an engineering director said once, 'My people know if they are doing a good job – because I'll tell them if they are not.' There is substantial evidence of 'negativity bias' in humans. Our attention is automatically drawn to negative information more strongly than it is automatically drawn to positive information (Wagner and Harter, 2006). However, emphasis on the negative so much more than the positive can be damaging, as the second piece of research from education shows.

A 1925 study conducted by Dr Elizabeth Hurlock in the USA examined the impact that different types of feedback would have on the performance of fourth- and sixth-year students in a maths class (Rath and Clifton, 2004). They were divided into three groups. In one they were publicly praised, in the second they were publicly criticized for poor work and in the third they were ignored. By the fifth day the overall improvement by group was:

- praised – 71 per cent;
- criticized – 19 per cent;
- ignored – 5 per cent.

To bring this more up to date and back to the workplace, the relatively new area of positive psychology has found that there is an ideal ratio of positive to negative interactions of 5:1. A workplace study found that teams where the ratio of positive to negative interactions was more than 3:1 had greater productivity than the work groups with a lower ratio.

Recognition and engagement

One of the earliest published pieces of work that showed a causal link between employee engagement and financial impact was in the

1990s at Sears Roebuck in the USA (Rucci *et al*, 1998). Specifically, they found that an increase in the employee attitude score by 5 points resulted in a customer satisfaction score increase of 1.3 points, which led to revenue growth of 0.5 per cent. This may not be surprising as we understand that the way organizations treat their employees is likely to have a direct impact on how employees treat customers. We all know that after a poor customer service experience, unless we have no choice, we will vote with our feet and buy elsewhere.

There is now considerable evidence to show that there is a correlation between engaged employees and organizational performance. Improving engagement also correlates with improving performance. Much of the evidence is summarized very effectively in the 2009 MacLeod report to government (MacLeod and Clark, 2009). Let me give you four examples from the report.

- In 2006 Gallup analysed 23,910 business units in different countries and found that those in the top half of engagement scores had 27 per cent higher profitability than those in the bottom half. The more highly engaged employees took an average of 2.7 days' sickness a year compared with disengaged employees, who took an average of 6.2 days a year.
- A 2006 international Gallup study of 89 companies found that the earnings-per-share growth of companies with engagement scores in the top quartile was 2.6 times that of organizations with below-average engagement scores.
- In 2007 Standard Chartered Bank found that branches around the world with a statistically significant increase in levels of employee engagement had a 16 per cent higher profit-margin growth than branches with decreased levels of employee engagement.
- Companies' products or services would be recommended by 78 per cent of engaged employees compared with only 13 per cent of the disengaged.

The 2007 YouGov People Index sampled some 40,000 people in the UK and found that there were five core factors that drive employee engagement. These hold true across organizations in different sectors, across large and smaller companies and at various stages of the employee life cycle:

- Recognition. Managers and the company make people feel valued when they have done a great job and celebrate their success.
- Reward. Do employees see a fair effort–reward balance?
- Change management. How effective are communications on change and do they engage employees in the change process?
- Performance management. How companies deal with poor performers and rewarding great performance.
- Leadership. Vision and strategy: managers engage and lead by example in terms of values and behaviours.

Based on a huge amount of research, Gallup have developed an engagement survey of just 12 questions, the Gallup Q12. Gallup believe that the Q12 gives a very clear and real view of the levels of engagement in an organization and highlights the critical dimensions. They have evidence showing increased sales and profit and lower employee turnover correlated with higher engagement scores measured by the Q12. One of the Q12 questions is: 'In the last seven days, I have received recognition or praise for doing good work.' It is also one of the six most powerful of the 12 questions, those with a combination of the strongest links to the most business outcomes (Buckingham and Coffman, 1999).

The criticality of employee engagement has now come to the top of the HR agenda. A 2010 survey of HR professionals in the UK found that employee engagement was their number one priority. Among the respondents, 55 per cent were measuring engagement and 88 per cent were trying to improve it (*The State of Human Resources Survey*, 2010).

Engagement is important and recognition is a critical element of engagement. It is also one that an organization can do something about relatively easily and cheaply compared with many of the other components of employee engagement.

Recognition in organizations

Gallup have done some substantial work on examining engagement within organizations. They have surveyed over 4 million employees worldwide. Their analysis of more than 10,000 business units and over 30 industries (Rath and Clifton, 2004) has found that individuals who receive regular recognition and praise:

- increase their individual productivity;
- increase their engagement among their colleagues;
- are more likely to stay with their organization;
- receive higher loyalty and satisfaction scores from their customers;
- have better safety records and fewer accidents on the job.

There are very many pieces of research across organizations that have found recognition to be a very significant factor, such as:

- A research project covering 5,000 US employees at all levels found that 70 per cent wanted specific individual recognition for a job well done (Wall and Jeffries quoted in Hale and Maehling, 1993).
- A survey of 1,500 US employees found that the number one workplace motivator was recognition. Specifically, the top motivator was personal congratulations from the manager for a job well done, which should be immediate and specific (Caudron, 1995).
- A survey of companies across eight countries found that praise was ranked as the top motivator of front-line employees, just ahead of money and time off (The Ascent Group, 2009).
- The Roffey Park Management Institute 2007 annual survey of managers in UK organizations, *The Management Agenda*, examined the motivation of managers. It found that the fourth biggest motivator was recognition by others. The third biggest demotivator was a lack of recognition.

In a survey by International Survey Research reported in Syedain (1995), the first three job priorities for UK workers were:

- being treated with fairness and respect;
- job security;
- recognition for good performance.

Of the people surveyed, 70 per cent said that recognition was 'very important' but only 37 per cent were satisfied with the recognition they get. This was the widest discrepancy among the 12 job priorities polled.

Happiness

A YouGov survey in the UK of over 4,000 working people found that the most impactful factor on the level of happiness employees had with their employer was recognition; yet it was one of the least favoured by employers (*Employee Benefits*, 2007). Recognition was identified as the most critical improvement area. The study showed that the majority of British employees did not believe that their employers were doing enough in recognition. Therefore, improving levels of recognition would be expected to increase employee happiness. The study concludes that 'Those employers which deliver will find they have a much happier, motivated and committed workforce on their hands and are more likely to reap productivity gains.'

Disengagement

A lack of effective recognition when people have really put themselves out can cost an organization in many different ways, as the following quote illustrates:

> Recently we were very busy and a few of us worked a lot of hours to help out, but you didn't get any thanks for it. We're just not appreciated at work. If someone were looking for a job, I wouldn't tell them to get one where I work.
>
> Susan, 43, customer service representative; *Working Life: Employee Attitudes and Engagement*, CIPD, 2006

When someone feels like Susan does in the quote above, they will lose pride in their organization. Instead of being an ambassador for their company they can be turned into a detractor. And all for the sake of a few words of thanks and genuine appreciation. It doesn't take much. With poor recognition, employees may not encourage others to join the organization, but they may also be more likely to leave. The US Department of Labor reports that the number one reason why people leave their job is because they 'do not feel appreciated' (Rath and Clifton, 2004).

National awards

National honours

Most of the examples in this book are about recognition and non-cash awards within organizations. But we also have very well-established systems of recognition in UK society. You find similar national recognition in many other countries, it is so important. The one that might spring to mind is the national honours system. This might be considered to be 'the nation's way of saying thank you'. Originally solely a gift of the sovereign, since 1993 any member of the public can write in to nominate someone for a national honour. Twice a year citizens are selected for an honour based on their achievements or their delivery of great service to the nation.

Normally people do not know that they have been nominated and fewer than 2 per cent refuse an honour when offered. Although the reasons vary, for at least some it is because they believe that they do not merit the honour for themselves as it was a team effort. In many cases, though, the recognition of the individual reflects across the organization. For example, a school will usually take great pride in an honour being bestowed on one of its teachers. Honours are well publicized, with the national and local media covering national and local figures who have been honoured. It is often the stories of the unsung heroes that are featured and are found to be so moving.

When they are asked as part of the process if they would help promote the honours system, some 85 per cent of people agree. Many people write to or telephone the Cabinet Office, who are responsible for the honours system, to express their pleasure and surprise that they have been honoured. It is clear that there is huge pride taken by the recipients of national honours as well as thanks and pride in the communities to which the recipients belong. But there is, of course, no tangible reward in receiving a national honour; simply the pride in the recognition from the nation for what you have done.

Armed forces

The armed forces recognize people by the use of orders, decorations and medals in three main categories: campaign, long service and gallantry.

Campaign medals

Campaign medals are awarded to members of the armed forces for their service in a particular operational theatre. They are awarded for being in the operation and do not normally distinguish between people's roles and precise location and perhaps degree of risk. The lines are often rather too blurred, so rather reinforce that the individuals are 'all of one company', all together in a campaign and have to rely on each other to achieve their operational aims.

Long service medals

Long service medals are awarded for long service and good conduct for those below officer level for 15 years of service. The medals are prized and there may be some small ceremony.

Gallantry medals

The gallantry medals are the most well known and high profile. They rank from the Victoria Cross through to a number of other medals all awarded for acts of gallantry. This may have been when the individual's life was at risk but they acted in a selfless manner to help save or defend others. Nominations are initiated from the bottom up and go through various groups who determine what level of medal, if any at all, should be awarded. The individual is told only a day or so before it is announced publicly. On the rare occasions when one of the rarest highest medals, the Conspicuous Gallantry Cross or even the Victoria Cross, is awarded, it receives major national coverage in the media. There have been only 13 VCs and 41 CGCs awarded since the end of the Second World War.

National honours, armed forces

In addition to the three categories mentioned, national honours are also awarded to members of the armed forces to recognize meritorious service. For example, the Order of the British Empire is used regularly as well as on operations to recognize those 'whose specific achievement or contribution goes further than is normally expected and clearly marks them out from their peers'.

Country support

Citizens of the country are generally very positive and supportive about this sort of national recognition. The underlying principles can be used in organizations and we should not be shy to use them. We also understand that in a national system, not everyone can be recognized by receiving an award or medal. This can lead to questions of fairness and equity, but not very ·many. Winston Churchill understood this balance well when he said the following in the House of Commons in March 1944:

> The object of giving medals, stars and ribbons is to give pride and pleasure to those who have deserved them. At the same time a distinction is something which everyone does not possess. If all have it, it is of less value. There must, therefore, be heartburnings and disappointments on the border line. A medal glitters, but it also casts a shadow. The task of drawing up regulations for such awards is one which does not admit of a perfect solution. It is not possible to satisfy everybody without the risk of satisfying nobody. All that is possible is to give the greatest satisfaction to the greatest number and to hurt the feelings of the fewest. But that is a most difficult task and it is easy to err on one side or the other. One must be careful in the first place to avoid profusion. The tendency to expand – shall I say inflate, dilute the currency through generous motives – is very strong.

Conclusions

Recognition is an important and enduring element in motivating people at work. It is part of the core of our society. Effective recognition can help:

- improve engagement and motivation;
- reduce absence;
- reduce employee turnover;
- improve productivity.

So the real question is: How can we use recognition to improve the motivation and retention of people in the organization? Much of the rest of this book tries to help answer this question.

KEY JOBS TO DO

- Research any of the motivation theories you have found interesting.
- Look up the MacLeod review http://www.berr.gov.uk/policies/employment-matters/strategies/employee-engagement.
- Identify arguments and evidence presented that you can use to help sell a recognition strategy to your organization.
- Consider where the links might be between employee engagement and organizational aims.

Chapter three
What and when should you recognize?

> *People respond to something that costs little or nothing, and that something is called recognition.*
>
> **ED LAWLER**

THIS CHAPTER COVERS

- What sorts of things can and should you recognize?
- What is the most effective frequency of recognition?

What to recognize

Recognition and incentives

As opposed to a performance-related pay system or cash-based incentive plan, a non-cash recognition programme awards things that are not dependent on achievement against a given target. Recognition programmes typically seek to recognize behaviours that fulfil overall values, such as excellent customer service, but are difficult if not impossible to record in terms of objectives – even if it was desirable to do so. It may be difficult to define precisely the behaviour that will be recognized, for example in the area of customer service, in particular given the emphasis on empowerment, but it might be captured in the phrase, 'I'll know it when I see it.' This is not to say that a recognition programme should be unfocused, simply that it is not an incentive scheme.

That said, although a recognition programme is very different from an incentive programme, some organizations blur the edges so that there are some programmes that 'recognize specific performance'. In these cases the relationship can look as shown in Figure 3.1.

FIGURE 3.1   Relationship between recognition schemes and incentive schemes

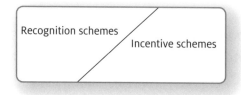

But in this chapter I deal with what sort of things to recognize and leave the incentive model until Chapter 8.

Guidelines

I ran a survey a few years ago of major private sector companies, and found that most organizations give fairly loose guidelines of what should be recognized. Examples include:

- 'excellent customer service';
- 'something over and above the norm';
- 'innovation, improvements, suggestions';
- 'exceptional contribution and teamwork'.

KPMG encourage people to recognize each other under one of the following:

- a great win;
- consistently outstanding performance;

- great teamwork;
- knowledge sharing;
- outstanding client service;
- problem solving;
- working across disciplines;
- leadership;
- corporate social responsibility;
- innovation;
- diversity.

In Chapter 10 you will see that a number of the other case study organizations (eg Comet, Prudential, Sky) give guidelines of what to recognize.

A common approach is for the recognition programme to be used to recognize something 'over and above the call of duty'. However, an alternative approach is to use it simply to reinforce good norms of behaviour. For example, Boyle (1995) describes a US programme introduced primarily to redress the balance between praise and criticism within the organization and to improve communications. The programme was based on a system of points, the '100 Club', which provided points for doing what was always expected but was often failed on, such as good attendance, punctuality, productivity, safety. The extrinsic value of the points was low but the symbolic value was high, as they were a manifestation of management's thanks.

You can give guidelines on what should be recognized but you cannot either mandate or give precise definitions. This inevitably means that some parts of the organization will use it more and use it for some behaviours; others will use it less, or not at all, and for slightly different things. You need to be able to live with this difference. If you are to encourage a culture of recognition and thanks you will also need to live with what might be seen as some inconsistency of application.

Values

An organization that has developed values may want to encourage people to recognize others who are clearly living the corporate values. A number of the case study organizations, including Edexcel, Prudential and Standard Chartered, use recognition to support and help drive their desired values and behaviours. Edexcel, for example, has 'Star Value Awards', which are for managers to use to recognize people whose actions or behaviours exceed expectations and embody the corporate values. You will see that such companies typically communicate widely the sorts of things people have done to be recognized in terms of values and behaviours to help others understand what they really mean. This approach converts something that might be a little remote and abstract into something real, using stories of what real people in the organization have done to illustrate what values really look and feel like.

Customer service

Excellent customer service is often recognized, particularly in the retail, hotel and catering sectors. Companies in these sectors often have well-developed recognition programmes that reflect excellence in customer service. The recognition might be initiated by a customer using some form of nomination process, the manager or a peer observing great service, or a mystery shopper programme. Case study organizations Comet, GOSH and Haringey Council all recognize customer service nominated by peers, managers or customers.

Mystery shoppers are now well used in the service sector to check on the level of customer service directly through the experience of an individual customer. Loch Fyne, the UK-based restaurant chain, now part of Greene King plc, uses mystery shoppers who report on each restaurant each quarter. The mystery shopper score is a component of the manager's bonus. A restaurant that scores highly receives a certificate, which might show, for example, that the restaurant scored 100 per cent for the last quarter in its mystery shopper score. The certificate is prominently displayed for customers to see and is a source of pride for the whole team working in the restaurant.

Internal customers

People working in some areas within an organization may be more likely to have the opportunity to display the sort of behaviours that are recognized – eg customer facing. It is important to understand this and ensure that everyone, not just the high-profile functions, can be recognized for the things they do. So if you want to use a recognition programme to help support great customer service, make sure you define it as applying to both internal and external customers – anyone in the value chain.

Failure

Failure may seem like a very strange thing to recognize. But how can organizations become leading edge unless they take risks that sometimes fail? If you do not fail you may well not be pushing the boundaries. In the pharmaceutical and IT sectors, for example, failure is constant. It may become an important part of the culture. So celebrate successes, but also accept and maybe encourage and recognize failure.

The leader of one US organization I came across wants to encourage his people to take risks, as he knows that that is the only way for his business to be successful. He also knows that with risk taking comes failure as well as success. To try to help encourage a risk-taking, no-blame culture, he regularly gives out $100 (£67) to anyone who has failed with a development. This is, of course, symbolic and underlying it is an understanding that the people in the organization are engaged and want to do the best job they can.

Health and safety

Health and safety issues may need to be considered in what to recognize. An employee may do something great, showing a real sense of customer service, but does it conform to appropriate health and safety guidelines? It would be giving the wrong message if you recognize someone who puts himself at risk inappropriately. This can be a very difficult issue to manage – because if you empower people, then they will make their own decisions. But it can put the individual and the organization at risk.

Recognizing management

As I cover in Chapter 4, managers need as much recognition as everyone else. A particularly interesting element of this may be recognizing managers for the effectiveness of their people management, as the following example illustrates.

Part of insurance group RSA's engagement strategy in the UK is to recognize their top-performing leaders. So in January 2010 they invited to a special dinner 100 people leaders from all job levels and parts of the UK business who either had one of the top engagement scores for their team or who had made the biggest improvement in their grand mean scores since the previous engagement survey.

The dinner was held at a prestigious restaurant in the City of London and was hosted by the UK CEO. Every member of the UK executive team attended and hosted a table. The event was featured on the intranet and in the RSA internal magazines. RSA wanted to make a big splash with this to show they recognized people leaders as role models to be emulated by others. The first event received extremely positive feedback from the attendees and is now run annually in the UK. Other regions in RSA are looking to replicate this.

Long service

Many organizations recognize long service. Within certain limits, covered in Chapter 6, Her Majesty's Revenue and Customs (HMRC) in the UK allow tax concessions for long service awards of at least 20 years and every 10 years thereafter. However, these sorts of length of service are becoming much less common than they were and will continue to reduce. The demise of defined benefit pensions that encouraged longer service, the faster pace of change and the expectations of generation Y all point to shorter service. It is said that the most important thing that a new graduate is looking for in their first job is the experience to build their CV for their second.

It is common for organizations to talk about the importance to them of individual and team performance and engagement. Although they rarely talk about the importance of long service, they continue to reward and recognize it. While I do not think that long service should necessarily be ignored, I do encourage organizations to question why they continue to recognize it and how the message carried by that recognition fits with their stated culture. I believe that in many cases long service is recognized because it always has been. One organization I spoke with said that long service was recognized as their performance management system was so effective that anyone who had achieved long service must also have performed well over the period, otherwise they would not still be employed.

Organizations in sectors that have particularly high turnover, such as catering – some over 100 per cent a year – do recognize relatively short service, such as a year or even six months. But that is of real demonstrable value to them and will fit their culture. Long service in the terms that most organizations would understand may be of little or no relevance to such companies.

Comet ensure that their managers have the start date and birthdays of the people in their team, so that they can recognize these events if they wish. This may be a very low-key recognition, but it does emphasize the individual.

In the public sector, in some sectors such as the police, long service is celebrated because it is part of the culture. The Metropolitan Police, for example, have regular presentations by the commissioner of long service and good conduct medals and certificates of long and meritorious service. Medals are presented to police officers and certificates to civilian staff. This was for 22 years' service until it was changed to 20 years in 2010. At a presentation in 2010, the commissioner, Sir Paul Stephenson, talked of how 'experience and maturity make a difference'. In the programme for the presentation was the following message from the commissioner:

Public service is a privilege and a calling. As Albert Einstein said, 'Only a life lived for others is a life worthwhile' and you have lived your life in the service of others. This is a celebration of your exemplary 22 years' service to your fellow citizen, performing a critical role in delivering safety and security for all of London's communities, and exercising the privilege of affecting their lives for the better, particularly when they most need our help. You can be proud of being part of an organization that is recognized throughout the world as representing the very best of policing. Your dedication, professionalism and hard work over the years have helped to maintain the finest traditions of our service and I am privileged, as your commissioner, to honour you today.

The message here is very different from what most private sector organizations might contrive to say about long service.

Suggestion schemes

HMRC also provide some tax concessions, within limits, as will be discussed in Chapter 6, for payments made for ideas that lead to improvements to the organization. It seems fair that if someone comes up with an idea that is typically outside what their job is about and that leads to a change that saves the organization money, they should get a share. This is what is behind the tax concessions. I referred above to a non-cash recognition programme called the 100 Club, operated by some US companies. Those companies using this non-cash points-based system had a very significantly higher number of suggestions being made and being implemented than the US companies not operating the scheme. I refer to this further in Chapter 6.

A points-based system works well as a system to recognize suggestions. A modest number of points can be given for any suggestion, with an increasing number for those shortlisted and again for those implemented.

But of course, like everything else, the culture of the organization must be right for such an approach to work. Although we have moved a very long way from the old command-and-control style of management, managers must see suggestions for improvements as a positive, as a strong sign of engagement and not a threat to their position. Otherwise people soon get the message, no matter what the signs on the noticeboard say about encouraging suggestions.

Comet have built a culture of recognition. They get some 1,000 suggestions a year within their 'Bright Sparks' suggestion scheme from their 10,000 employees.

When to recognize people

Evidence presented in Chapter 2 shows that recognition is important in the motivation and engagement of people. Further work based on Skinner considered what was the most effective frequency of reinforcement. Four main frequencies were examined:

- Variable ratio. Reinforcement is delivered at random intervals, so that the individual does not know when this might happen.
- Fixed ratio. Reinforcement is every nth response. For example, a salesperson gets a £1,000 ($1,500) bonus for every 10 sales.
- Variable interval. Reinforcement is for the first response after a random average length of time since the last reinforcement. For example, an award every few days, which is three days on average.
- Fixed interval. Reinforcement for the first response only after a fixed length of time; for example, a weekly prize.

The research shows that variable random reinforcement is much more effective than reinforcement that is time bound or linked to frequency. That is not to say that time-bound recognition and reinforcement, such as employee of the month, will not work. It may well do, but random reinforcement is likely to be more effective. This does suggest that if you want to make maximum impact and get the greatest return for your expenditure, look at the local immediate plans first.

Immediate recognition

Companies usually formally reward employees based on a 12-monthly cycle, typically related to the financial year. The emphasis on the annual cycle may come from the management-by-objectives school and the need for the organization to manage its processes within a budgeting cycle using a centrally administered process. But results and achievement do not necessarily fit neatly into this cycle, which in individual performance terms is for many people somewhat arbitrary. But as part of a true culture of performance management, more regular recognition opportunities need to be part of the whole process.

One of the advantages of recognition programmes over other parts of the reward package, particularly at the more informal end of the spectrum, is that they can allow immediate recognition of behaviour. Recognition should be both immediately after the event and spontaneous – the surprise adds to the power of the recognition.

If you want to minimize the time lag between the accomplishment and the award, then a decentralized approach is critical. Initial recognition must be immediate and if you have other levels of programmes to recognize people at a corporate level, then you still need to minimize the time period between the action and the more formal recognition as far as you can. Recognition programmes should reflect the reality of performance, not the administrative requirements.

Longer-term programmes

In my survey, respondents said that their recognition programmes were designed for recognizing people on the following frequency:

- any time: 46 per cent;
- monthly: 20 per cent;
- quarterly: 4 per cent;
- annually: 30 per cent.

Typically, the more frequent awards were more informal and local and the more infrequent were more formal and corporate. There may be some duplication here, in that some companies reported a single programme that might have two levels, for example a monthly award that qualified the nominee for an annual award as well.

Recognition should not be a zero-sum game. You cannot limit recognition by quota or budget or time. The most important thing is to recognize the great things people do when they do them. But you may want to add recognition programmes that cover a longer period later on.

Although I advocate the value of local informal immediate recognition, some organizations wish to have higher-profile and hence longer-term programmes. These are discussed in Chapter 4.

KEY JOBS TO DO

- Review what you should encourage to be recognized, based on your culture and aims.
- Consider how you can maximize the impact of recognition by using variable random recognition.

Chapter four
How should you recognize people?

Catch people doing something right.

BLANCHARD AND JOHNSON (1993) *THE ONE MINUTE MANAGER*

THIS CHAPTER COVERS

- recognition as a continuum: day to day, informal, formal;
- the importance of recognition by the manager;
- how to recognize day to day;
- the essence of celebration;
- non-cash ideas to support recognition;
- how to avoid creating losers from winners.

Introduction

Recognition can be very low-key day-to-day or high-profile corporate events. In fact, it is best to think of it as a continuum, as shown in Figure 4.1.

FIGURE 4.1 Recognition

| Day to day | Local, informal, low key, simple | Corporate, formal, high profile |

Day-to-day recognition can be just the simple thanks for a job well done. It is really just the normal courtesy one might expect. It is about not taking people or what they do for granted. It may be just an oral thanks or perhaps a written thank-you note. It is not time bound. Standard Chartered have a well-developed approach that incorporates this.

Informal recognition is likely to identify an individual or team for special praise that is publicly given. It may have a small non-cash award attached sourced by the manager or through the organization's third-party supplier. Celebrations will be local and fairly low key and low cost. It will be much less structured than formal recognition. Any publicity is likely to be within the division or department, although sometimes it may go across the organization. It is not likely to be time bound. KPMG have their 'Menu of recognition' that allows managers to buy fairly low-value gifts to present to people locally.

Formal recognition will be some form of structured programme for the whole division or organization. It may be based on corporate values or behaviours and is likely to involve some forms of time-bound nominations, selection and formal presentation of a certificate and non-cash award, most likely in a formal setting. There is likely to be publicity across the organization.

Many organizations develop a series of recognition programmes to try and drive recognition throughout the organization. These may cover the whole continuum.

Who values receiving recognition most?

Organizational level

Evidence presented in Chapter 2 shows how recognition can be a critical, and often missing, motivator for people at work. But is recognition important for certain groups?

Herzberg (1959) found that those of high rather than low educational levels more frequently cited recognition as a motivating factor. Recognition was more frequently cited by those high in the organization rather than at a lower level.

On the other hand, those people occupying the least skilled, lowest paid and perhaps most undervalued jobs may particularly value recognition. The CEO of a residential maid service in the USA said that 'many of our workers have never known respect and getting it changes them for the better'. Rosalind Jeffries, president of Performance Enhancement Group, a US HR consulting firm, says, 'People at the lower [wage] levels beg for the intangibles – the pat on the back, the verbal thank you. Self-esteem is a little lower, and they want to know they're OK' (Maynard, 1997).

The importance of recognition as a motivator is enduring. Tulgan (1996) argues that recognition is vital for managing and motivating the so-called Generation X, typically defined as those born from the early 1960s to the end of the 1970s. Ipsos MORI conducted a survey on the attitudes of Generation Y – those born in the 1980s and 1990s (*Personnel Today*, September 2008). The survey found that the three most important job factors for this group were (showing the total positive scores):

- holiday entitlement: 87 per cent;
- recognition for good work: 86 per cent;
- salary/bonus: 85 per cent.

The three least important job factors were:

- international travel: 19 per cent;
- gym membership: 18 per cent;
- season ticket loan: 11 per cent.

This survey suggests that you need to give Generation Y a decent salary and bonus and enough holiday, but your priority should be effective recognition, which may cost nothing, before spending money on things like gym membership and season ticket loans.

It is more common to find recognition programmes in retail, hotel and catering, leisure, transport and service businesses, primarily because of the high customer interface. Organizations frequently use non-cash recognition to support customer service. But as the range of case study organizations shows, recognition can be used in any organization.

Conclusion

My conclusion from all of the research and evidence is that recognition is important to everyone, be they the chief executive or the most lowly paid manual worker, whether they have two PhDs or no qualifications, whether they work in the service sector or manufacturing, whether they are coming up to retirement or have just started their career. What is important is that the way in which they are recognized may be different.

Teams or individuals

My survey found that 49 per cent of the programmes reported were designed for recognizing either teams or individuals, 46 per cent for recognizing individuals only, and 5 per cent were for teams only. However, a number of respondents said that in practice awards are mostly given to individuals and not teams.

Recognition can be used very effectively to celebrate and acknowledge the achievement of a whole team. Given the amount of project team working in most organizations, it would seem obvious to find ways to celebrate their achievements and successes.

Non-cash recognition for the whole team could complement a performance pay system that rewards individuals. When a team of employees achieves, the entire team needs to be recognized. If only the manager or highest performer is recognized, the team can lose motivation (Nelson, 1994).

Most of the case study organizations cover both teams and individuals. In a number of cases, such as BIS, KPMG and Prudential, they have a particular award for teams. This can take the form of a team event rather than a tangible award to individual team members.

National differences

Following Herzberg's original study in the USA in the 1950s, other researchers undertook similar studies in both the USA and other countries. Although achievement or recognition were the first factors in studies in the USA, studies in Finland, Hungary, New Zealand and Latin America found different leading motivating factors. Other research showed that other nationalities cited hygiene factors as satisfiers more frequently than did the Americans in the same sample (Steers and Porter, 1991). This suggests that the factors that are most significant in motivation may be related to national culture, so that it would be inappropriate to assume that Herzberg's theory can be applied universally. But perhaps we should consider Maslow's hierarchy, which suggests that the lower-level needs must be met before the esteem need will be effective. In some developing countries many people may be more concerned about basic needs first.

Standard Chartered Bank, who operate in over 70 countries, have found that there is a positive correlation between employee engagement and a range of financial and customer measures everywhere. For example, in India there was a considerably lower employee turnover in the most engaged compared with the least engaged employees. In Hong Kong new sales growth in a branch was higher where the employees were highly engaged compared with a branch with lower levels of employee engagement. In Korea there were lower losses in branches with the most engaged employees.

A study by HRM Singapore in 2005 found that when the 3,000 people interviewed were asked the question, 'What do you really want from your job?', recognition was second after career/learning development opportunities, with pay third (Gostick and Elton, 2007).

Wagner and Harter (2006) give a case study of how effective recognition was in changing a business in Poland.

To the extent to which recognition is a component of employee engagement, this suggests that recognition is likely to have an impact in most if not all countries.

Who should do the recognizing?

My survey found that 64 per cent of the recognition programmes reported were designed for the manager to recognize their people,

13 per cent were for colleagues to recognize each other and 23 per cent were for a variety of people. To build a culture of appreciation and recognition you may well build a series of programmes as I discuss below. So to summarize, there are probably three groups who could do the recognizing:

- the individual's manager;
- the individual's colleagues;
- the individual's customers.

Recognition as a management practice

The everyday

Recognition starts at the day-to-day level – really the manager saying 'thank you' – and goes up to very formal corporate programmes. Armstrong (1996) states that 'recognition is also provided by managers who listen to and act upon suggestions of their team members and, importantly, acknowledge their contribution'. Johnson and Redmond (1998) believe that 'A sense of recognition comes about when people are called by their names, when their opinion is valued and their queries or comments are treated seriously.'

Evidence

There is very considerable evidence that the immediate line manager has huge impact on the motivation and engagement of people (MacLeod review, Standard Chartered, Gallup). For example, Gallup found that five factors consistently emerged from their focus groups and surveys:

- work environment and procedures;
- immediate supervisor;
- team/co-workers;
- overall company, senior management;
- individual commitment, service intention.

Of these five major factors, by far the most powerful was immediate supervisor (Buckingham and Coffman, 1999).

Blanchard and Johnson (1993) emphasize the importance of recognition to counter the common management attitude of being quick to criticize failure but slow to praise success, as covered in Chapter 2. They say that managers should 'Catch people doing something right.'

Lyons (2000) argues that there are seven core leadership skills that are vital for today's leaders in the post-factory setting. One of the essential seven is 'giving recognition': 'This is a powerful leadership activity that is not emphasized enough in traditional management styles, and is a key to making strategy work over time. The results that come from appropriate recognition of a job well done are extremely positive and motivational to both the individual and the team. Giving recognition can also be one of the easiest skills to coach.'

Based on their extensive research, Kouzes and Posner (2007) believe that there are 'five practices of exemplary leadership':

- Model the way.
- Inspire a shared vision.
- Challenge the process.
- Enable others to act.
- Encourage the heart.

On 'Encourage the heart' they say: 'Accomplishing extraordinary things in organizations is hard work. To keep hope and determination alive, leaders recognize contributions that individuals make. In every winning team, the members need to share in the rewards of their efforts, so leaders celebrate accomplishments. They make people feel like heroes.'

The low impact of corporate recognition

A study of 800 US healthcare workers by McCormick and Ilgen (La Motta, 1995) sought to identify the motivational impact of each of a number of recognition techniques using a four-quadrant model for analysis, as shown in Figure 4.2.

FIGURE 4.2   Four-quadrant analysis of recognition
techniques

	Company initiated	Manager initiated
Performance		Most motivating
Presence	Least motivating	

The study found that the most motivating techniques were manager initiated relating to performance. The least motivating related to recognition of presence (such as a birthday card), particularly when company initiated. Although the centrally produced birthday card may be efficient, it is not effective. This reinforces Herzberg's view that recognition is only of value when associated with achievement.

Understanding the individual

It is worth reflecting that people can feel recognized in many different ways. For many people, in particular top performers, increased responsibility and lessened supervision can be recognition in themselves. Alternatives may be additional time off or alternative assignments (Joinson, 1996). Empowerment can be a form of recognition to the extent that the individual is being given the tools and authority to achieve results. Empowerment means that a sense of trust must be present and implies that the individual's competence is recognized and appreciated.

Supporting managers

There is overall compelling evidence that the most important way to improve people's feeling of being recognized is by helping the managers and supervisors in the organization to do so. Standard Chartered and Comet, for example, do this. A common use of recognition programmes is to support managers and encourage the simple acknowledgement of the good things people do. So a recognition programme can be an important part of the 'kit bag' of processes and interventions available to managers.

How to do it

Key factors

Recognition can be orally and face to face, and ideally with something to remember; or it may be in writing. The big advantage of it being in writing is that it then provides the memory itself: the recipient can show their family and friends. Especially as almost all written communications nowadays are electronic, a handwritten note can work particularly well. But as mobile company 3 have found, a text message can be effective within the sort of population for whom this is the communication norm. But whatever the medium, this is what to aim for and how to do it:

- Be genuine: if you don't mean it, then don't say it.
- Be timely: make it as close to the event as you can.
- Be personal: use the person's name.
- Make it specific: refer to exactly what they did.
- Be clear: explain why it is appreciated.
- Make it public: find a way to let others know.

You may not manage to hit all six of these factors every time, but keep them all in mind and aim for as many as you can. But the one you need to ensure every single time is the first – be genuine. As Kouzes and Posner (2007) say, 'When people see a charlatan making noisy affectations, they turn away in disgust.'

Individuals are different

The form of the recognition will depend a lot on the individual. There is a danger that recognition by managers is in the form that they themselves would value, not necessarily what the recipient would appreciate. It is therefore important to first understand what makes people feel recognized. We really need to know how individuals operate to be able to know what form any recognition should take. For example, an introverted person may gain maximum reward from knowing in themselves that they have done a good job, whereas an extrovert type may require the recognition of others.

The key here is that one size does not fit all. Find out what is important to the individual and work on that. This goes both for the form of recognition and any non-cash that you use. So try to individualize both the recognition form and of course the award. This is one reason why the centralized programmes can be less effective than you might hope. If you try to shoehorn everyone through the same process, it will impact on some more positively than others. Some people will simply remove themselves from it. Some people may just value a quiet word one to one. Others may enjoy being called up on stage and applauded. Maybe someone is a bit reticent but will find that they do enjoy it after all. As one award recipient said, 'I had to go up on stage. It was a bit embarrassing but I did like it – you do feel a bit special.'

Sir John Harvey-Jones, chairman of ICI and business trouble-shooter on television, believed that 'The art of the unscheduled reward lies in the personalization of the reward and the manner of its giving, as much as its cash value' (1994). He went on to say that:

> Unscheduled rewards must be presented in ways which are public and overt. The fact that unscheduled rewards are made is in itself a message to all your people that you as a manager and the company as an organization are interested in individuals and individual performance, that you are close to what is going on, that it is appreciated and that this appreciation can take a tangible form.

Southwest Airlines in the USA have a simple guide to recognition that can be summarized in the following (Freiberg and Freiberg, 1996):

- Say 'thank you' often.
- Always celebrate people from the heart.
- Make heroes and heroines of employees who glorify your company's values.
- Find people who serve behind the scenes and celebrate their contributions.

- Create a celebration signature – balloons, photos, trophies.
- Celebrate at work like you do at home. Celebrate at home like Southwest does at work.

Peer recognition

Many organizations encourage anyone to recognize others as part of their approach to recognition. This may be in addition to a manager recognition programme or in isolation. Although research shows that manager recognition is likely to have the greatest impact on the engagement of people, peer recognition is another element of developing a culture of recognition throughout an organization.

An advantage of encouraging anyone to nominate someone is that it is likely to help build cooperation and team working. Some organizations particularly encourage people to recognize those in different departments but with whom they have regular contact – typically the internal customer. The role of managers has changed and with greater empowerment and flatter structures the manager may miss some of the great things people do every day. So a programme allowing recognition from anyone can really help to 'catch people doing something right'. Some of the most powerful recognition comes when someone (or more typically a team) nominates their boss for recognition.

The majority of the case study organizations have an element of peer recognition. This may be simply providing some form of card to encourage people to write a note of thanks or may involve a small non-cash award as part of the thanks.

Customer recognition

In addition to allowing people within the organization to recognize colleagues, some recognition programmes include other stake-holders such as suppliers, contractors and customers.

Many organizations, in particular in the hotel, catering and related service industries, have developed some form of award system based on nominations by customers. As customers, we are all familiar with the sort of forms we are encouraged to complete in hotels or on airlines or in restaurants. Nominations will often go to a panel for review and there may be a series of awards based on the nominations received over a period of time. Haringey Council's recognition programme uses the 'WOW! Awards', which only accept nominations from customers. Great Ormond Street Hospital for Children NHS Trust (GOSH) have a recognition programme with a number of categories, which include nominations from patients and their families.

More formal approaches

In addition to recognizing people individually in relatively low-key ways, you should also consider the more formal approaches. These are likely to have a more formal (but fun!) setting and are likely to have some publicity coverage about what people have done to receive the award.

The next step up from simple day-to-day recognition would be to formally present an individual with a recognition award at an existing event such as a department meeting, training or briefing session.

To raise the profile some more, lay on a special event locally, such as a buffet lunch, where the individual is presented with the award.

A corporate award programme may have a regular award ceremony – typically with lunch or dinner – where the winners are presented with their awards. This is often done by a senior person in the organization – ideally the chief executive. The people to be awarded are often able to invite people to the event, such as family or work colleagues.

Celebration

In each case you need to ensure an atmosphere of celebration. Southwest Airlines follow a number of common-sense guidelines that contribute to the success of celebrations in the company

(Freiberg and Freiberg, 1996). I think that this is an excellent summary of how any organization should look at how it celebrates:

- The celebration must be authentic – it must come from the heart.
- The celebration must raise people's dignity and self-respect – it must never harm.
- The celebration must be done right – it should be well coordinated, well timed and well executed in a quality way.
- The celebration must appeal to the senses – use balloons, banners, flags, costumes, videos and photographs.
- The celebration must be seen as an investment – it should not be seen as a cost.
- The celebration must be cost effective – look for the least expensive way to do it right.

Whether informal or formal, make it public. Harvey-Jones has said: 'One of the purposes of unscheduled rewards is to underscore public recognition in a way which passes a little bit of glory on to the individual who has won a reward' (1994). A ceremony should fit the culture of the organization. It does not need to be over-elaborate but should be a genuine celebration. It is common to take photographs at more formal ceremonies so that people have a memento of the occasion and that may be used in publicity. Organizations who use ceremonies do so in many different ways. Here are three examples, two of which are case study organizations.

The Metropolitan Police

The Metropolitan Police run three or four ceremonies a year to recognize and award those police officers receiving a commendation. They also run ceremonies every six weeks or so to recognize police and civilian staff achieving certain career milestones. Those being recognized are invited with their family and friends to attend the ceremony at the Peel Centre, the police training school in Hendon, North London. They are asked to bring no more than three guests, but may request to bring more family; their requests will be accommodated if space allows. The Simpson Hall, which is used for the ceremonies, can hold over 500 people. The commissioner himself attends every ceremony. After addressing the audience, he presents the medals and certificates; each presentation is photographed. He then remains after the ceremony to allow the recipients to have further photographs with him and their family. More than half of those attending do queue up for these family photographs. Following the address by the commissioner and the presentation, which lasts less than an hour, a buffet afternoon tea is available.

The commissioner emphasizes the critical role of the family in enabling those in the Met to be able to do their jobs. He says (to quote from a recent presentation), 'Thanks to all the family and friends who provide love, security and energy to help keep us going. We could not do our job without your support. If the medal was bigger we could have your names on it as well.' Although very well organized with the degree of precision you would expect of a uniformed service, there is also informality, mainly because of the large number of family members attending. The ceremony is about recognizing the individual and their family. It enables the family to share in the success of the person being recognized.

GOSH

Great Ormond Street Hospital have brought together the recognition of people in three categories – long service, achieving qualifications, and performance – into a single annual ceremony. Even so, they manage it so that it lasts less than 40 minutes. They know that although the celebration is important it can be done effectively and in the right spirit without dragging on. So they recognize people hitting a particular long service time (20 years, etc) as a group rather than each person individually. They hold the annual ceremony at 5 o'clock so that it fits in towards the end of a standard working day and can be accommodated between shifts. Photographs are taken and there is a reception after the ceremony.

Haringey Council

Haringey Council in London hold a short presentation of their WOW! Awards every six weeks or so for the latest winners. It is primarily the winners who attend, plus some other Haringey staff, so there may be around 30 or so people at the ceremony. Each individual is presented with their certificate by a councillor and has their photograph taken.

Cash versus non-cash

The four reasons

Cash has the advantage of being easy to administer – every organization already has a payroll, so why not just use it? Well, I gave four key reasons in Chapter 1:

- differentiation;
- memory value;
- perceived value;
- more personal.

For recognition, differentiation is the most important. A recognition programme is not a substitute for pay. What is important is the recognition itself, not the financial or non-cash award. Where awards are paid in cash – particularly through the payroll – they tend to be seen by managers as part of pay, and the more fundamental motivator of recognition of achievement can get lost. If you still insist in paying recognition awards through the payroll, then at least use the message space on most payslips for further congratulations.

Immediacy

Sir John Harvey-Jones believed in the value of what he termed 'non-systematic immediate awards' (1994). He argued that an immediate award of a few hundred pounds accompanied by appropriate thanks from the manager will have a much greater positive motivational effect and will cost much less than a salary increase at the end of the year. He also believed in the value of a tangible gift – referring to his own practice of sending cases of wine and thanks to people who have done something particularly meritorious. 'The essence of the reward is that it is a tangible way of saying thank you that is not put forward by the personnel department.'

Choice of award

Choice of award is important. If the aim is to maximize the perceived value to the recipient, then it is important to offer as much choice as possible. The size of any award must acknowledge the size of the deed. If the award is too small, it may trivialize the behaviour; if it is too large, it may cause a sense of unfairness. Any tangible component of recognition should be seen as worthy in the minds of the recipients, 'but it is also a symbol of recognition and has to be properly presented and delivered' (Bryant, 1994).

Different types of recognition programmes have quite different levels of awards. My survey of recognition programmes in major private sector companies some years ago found that they tended to cluster into two groups. First were the low-value, fairly informal awards that could be given fairly frequently. Most typically these were gifts, retail vouchers or dinner out with one's partner, with a value of £30 to £250 ($45 to $375). At the other extreme were the high-profile awards given annually. These were relatively high value and were commonly a holiday or other trip overseas or prizes/vouchers worth up to £4,000 ($6,000).

The essence of any recognition programme is to ensure that people are appropriately recognized for what they do. The components used are only a means, not the end. Pitts (1995) argues that it is important not to confuse the form of recognition with the fact. So although the US approach to the form of recognition programmes may not be felt to suit the more reserved British culture, recognition itself is equally important.

Non-cash award ideas

Take care

The choice of award is limited only by your imagination. But it is important to think carefully about the award and the individual.

A huge bunch of flowers may look great, but how do you get them home on a bus? So send the person home in a taxi. A food hamper may be well received, but it could flop if the recipient is a vegetarian. As discussed in Chapter 2, the choice of award can either build or damage your relationship. Your choice of award can carry the message that it is clear that you know the person well, or that you have got it completely wrong and it backfires. So choose carefully. That is why many organizations use a points-based online award system that allows the employee to make their own choice. But getting just the right thing can say so much more than some points.

Individual or family?

One aspect of the award you should consider is whether it should be for the individual alone or the family or the partner. Where the award is in part to reflect considerable extra time spent, for example to finish a project, you might want to provide something for the partner and perhaps children rather than just the individual. You are saying thank you to the family. It is usually appreciated. When someone works late or unsociable hours it is also the partner who suffers. As we saw earlier, the Metropolitan Police actively include the family in the presentations.

After a heavy storm, five male workers in a telephone company were sent out to do overnight repairs on Valentine's Day. As a form of thanks, each employee's spouse was sent a box of chocolates with a card expressing the company's appreciation for her husband's efforts (Nelson, 1994). It was really appreciated, not because of the value of the gift, but because the organization had gone to the trouble of acknowledging the situation.

Non-cash ideas

Here are a few ideas of non-cash awards to get you thinking:

- plaques or certificates;
- bottle of champagne;
- food hamper;

- house cleaning for a year;
- car parking for six months;
- the prime parking spot in the office car park for a month;
- dinner out for two;
- box at the theatre or opera;
- voucher for a family photograph;
- tickets to a sports event;
- cinema vouchers;
- personalized engraved items;
- a small number of shares or share options in the company;
- day off for the employee on their birthday;
- Fridays off in June;
- magazine subscription for a year;
- retail shop vouchers;
- charity donation;
- catered dinner at home by a chef;
- spa or health club day out;
- cooking lessons;
- weekend sports car/limousine hire;
- fruit basket;
- present for the employee's partner at the end of a lot of overtime.

A 2008 World at Work survey of US companies found that the types of items used as recognition awards were as shown in Table 4.1.

TABLE 4.1   Items used as recognition awards

	%
Certificates and/or plaques	78
Cash	60
Gift certificates for product purchases	51
Food (breakfast, lunch, pizza party, etc)	42
Timepieces (watches, clocks, etc)	30
Jewellery	28
Household items	26
Office accessories	25

TABLE 4.1   *Continued*

....

	%
Electronics (cameras, TVs, etc)	21
Recreational items/sporting goods	19
Gift certificates for personal services (spa treatments, etc)	17
Travel	15
Other	11

Make it fun

One big advantage of non-cash over cash is that non-cash can be public and you can more easily use it to generate a sense of fun. Gifts and awards do not need to be high value, but they can be fun. This can be particularly effective with something for a whole work group. Quite a few organizations say that 'fun' is one of their values. They understand that the whole person comes to work and that it is okay to have a laugh at work – we spend a huge proportion of our time at work so we should enjoy it. A light-hearted event can dissolve the daily tension (Hemsath and Yerkes, 1997).

This is something that can work well for small groups – but not at all easily for large corporate programmes. Managers should be able to find themes from time to time related to a product, service or event that can be reflected in a non-cash prize or gift.

Professionals and the highly paid

Some people think that non-cash awards will have less impact on the highly paid professional. 'They can buy any of this stuff themselves anyway, so why bother?' But remember two things. The tangible award is only part of the thanks; mostly you have to get the thanks right. But it is not pay. If you were to give £100 ($150) to someone earning £100,000 ($150,000) that would almost always be seen as trivial and not worthwhile, particularly if it was taxed as well. But if instead you gave them an expensive bottle of champagne and paid the tax on it, it might cost you a little more than £100 ($150) but its impact would be entirely different. There are a number of items in the ideas list above that would be appreciated by the highly paid. I am sure that you can see those that might be appropriate for some of your highly paid employees. But you might want to give it a bit more thought. So, if it is a bottle of champagne, make sure it is a decent bottle!

Creating winners, not losers

An individual being recognized may be motivated, but will it have a positive or negative effect on the rest of the population? There is a danger that highly publicized recognition programme awards can be divisive in that for all the winners there may be people who feel like losers.

Event based

The typical employee of the month programme, which may have a single winner, can create a winners-and-losers environment. This is particularly the case if it is seen that the individual chosen by management had not done anything particularly special, but was chosen as there needs to be a monthly winner – although there may be a different perception if chosen by customers or peers. But such a time-bound programme can damage effective team working.

You really should not limit recognition by a quota. In one organization where a formal programme was introduced to recognize outstanding performers, feedback showed that employees felt that the programme did not recognize enough people often enough (Hale and Maehling, 1993).

Mary Kay Cosmetics has a well-developed reward programme and is often recognized as one of the top 100 most motivating companies in the USA to work for (La Motta, 1995). There is a large range of non-cash awards available, up to pink Cadillacs, which are presented at the annual awards ceremony. There is no limit to the number of people who can receive the awards and therefore each person competes only with themselves and no others in the company.

So, as discussed in Chapter 3, it is better to make programmes event based rather than time bound, so that the number of winners is unlimited. This is one way to help avoid creating losers.

Nelson (1996) says that recognition is not just for the person who performed well, it is also a message to other employees about the type of performance that gets noticed in an organization. Kanter, quoted in Nelson (1996), says, 'To the rest of the organization, recognition creates role models and heroes and communicates the standards: these are the kinds of things that constitute great performance around here.'

Acceptability

If it is not clear to people why an individual has been chosen for a formal award, it can lead to dissatisfaction. In the absence of clear reasons, people will be guided by their own perceptions of the person (Hale and Maehling, 1993). 'Genuine recognition of performance is something people really appreciate. They will continue to support the [recognition] program, whether or not they, as individuals, participate in the awards' (Crosby, quoted in La Motta, 1995).

Fairness and acceptability are vital to a successful programme. Therefore a challenge is to ensure that awards go only to those individuals whose achievements are of such a magnitude that they are recognized by superiors, subordinates and peers. Although an individual may feel that he should have received an award, he will not quibble about someone else's (Friedson, 1985).

When I was reviewing one organization's recognition programme, I came across a number of people who had received an award but were embarrassed about it because they saw that the award was undeserved, as they had done nothing special. On investigation it appeared that the awards were being used by managers as a form of pay rather than recognition, which had the result of devaluing the whole programme. This illustrates Herzberg's view that recognition without achievement is trivial.

One of the changes that was introduced to improve this programme was that for the higher level of award a group of previous winners with a cross section of people in the business was used as the 'judging panel'. The selection was therefore now made by people's colleagues rather than higher management. This is something I would suggest any organization considers. Using previous winners will not only help validate the decisions but will also ensure greater transparency. Previous winners are not usually soft judges. You are likely to find that the standards associated with awards are maintained.

Allocation of awards

Where a tangible award is being used to support recognition, some organizations use a draw to find the winner. This means that no one has been selected out and becomes a loser. They all have an equal chance to get the prize. The other advantage of this approach to the organization is that you can budget exactly.

Language

Another approach to minimize the winner/loser effect is the way you use language. Even if there is to be one main award, do you need to call the recipient the winner? Great Ormond Street Hospital want to celebrate all of those being recognized. Conscious of the danger of creating losers, at their presentations and subsequent publicity, the words 'winner' and 'runners-up' are not used. Rather, there are typically two people named as 'shortlisted' and then, 'the person receiving the award is ...'.

Series of programmes

Ideally recognition should 'touch' as many people as possible. There is, however, the danger that if one programme is used much too widely then its value can be diluted. Therefore organizations need to consider this balance. But as I have said before, you cannot restrict the recognition of people to a quota.

Although organizations often start with one type of approach to recognition – and I advocate starting with the simple day-to day-thanks that could potentially touch anyone and everyone – they also often build a series of programmes and approaches across the continuum. There can be different reasons for this. But formal recognition programmes usually cover only a small number of people. Other programmes and approaches can therefore be used to find different ways to recognize people in the organization.

A number of the case study organizations have a series of programmes covering different aspects. For example, 3 has 'Thank you' cards, 'Round of applause' and 'Oscars@3'. Edexcel has 'Star cards', 'Star Value Awards' and 'Star Exceptional Awards'.

KEY JOBS TO DO

- Consider how you can build recognition as a management practice.
- Review the nature of celebratory events.
- Implement strategies to avoid creating losers.
- Find ways to use more team recognition.

Chapter five
Designing your recognition programme

Because of its power, ridiculously low cost and rarity, [recognition] is one of the greatest lost opportunities in the business world today.

WAGNER AND HARTER (2006)
12: THE ELEMENTS OF GREAT MANAGING

THIS CHAPTER COVERS

- defining recognition objectives and what success will look like;
- using employee engagement surveys;
- building a series of recognition programmes;
- using third-party providers;
- reviewing your programmes.

Defining objectives and successful outcomes

Introduction

Before you do anything else, you need to be clear about why you want to introduce a recognition programme. Like any other HR strategy, a recognition programme will not be effective if it is simply grafted on to the existing processes. Before introducing a new programme, carefully consider what it is trying to achieve and the context within which it will be introduced. A programme needs to fit the organizational culture and values.

A recognition programme will not work in isolation with a demotivated and disengaged workforce; it has to be part of a whole culture of valuing people. There is a danger that by introducing a recognition programme, managers may believe that you have dealt with recognition rather than them having to do too much. But people recognize other people and managers in particular need to do this. Just because you have a recognition programme does not mean you have a culture of genuine recognition.

Appropriate aims

A 2008 World at Work survey of US organizations found that the objectives/goals for their recognition schemes were as shown in Table 5.1.

TABLE 5.1 Objectives/goals for recognition schemes

	%
Create a positive work environment	77
Motivate high performance	71
Create a culture of recognition	69
Recognize years of service	69
Increase morale	68
Reinforce desired behaviours	61

TABLE 5.1 *Continued*

	%
Support organizational mission/values	55
Increase retention or decrease turnover	51
Support becoming/remaining an employer of choice	43
Encourage loyalty	42
Provide line of sight to company goals	26
Support a culture change	20
Other	2

The survey I ran a few years ago found the top four reasons for introducing a recognition programme were:

- to recognize performance 'above and beyond';
- to improve customer service;
- to recognize achievement;
- to support line managers.

A while ago I worked with a public sector organization to review and relaunch their recognition programme. The purpose of the relaunched programme was defined as 'to recognize the behaviour of people in providing excellent customer service and/or support of colleagues over and above the norms of their job'.

The Co-operative Group introduced a new group-wide employee recognition scheme in November 2009 with the simple aim of improving employee engagement across the organization.

Best practice or best fit

Beware of what I call the 'golf club effect'. This is typically where the CEO calls you in after having played golf over the weekend with the CEO of Big Co who has recently implemented some sort of, in this case, recognition, programme. They may have, for example, an employee of the month or year award at which the CEO of Big Co has recently presented awards. He thought it was a good idea to help improve employee morale. 'Let's have one of those,' says your CEO. Three obvious points:

- There may be no evidence that the Big Co approach is working. Often such programmes are introduced as the CEO feels it better to be seen to do something about recognition.
- Even if it is having a positive impact at the moment, it may not have staying power. Such a programme is difficult to sustain as it can become difficult to keep finding people who deserve to win. The programme can become devalued.
- But more important than both of these is that just because one organization is doing something does not mean that it can simply be grafted to another.

You can quickly and easily introduce a recognition programme using some other organization's model. But rushing into action without careful thought and planning is likely to lead to long-term failure and a waste of money. A little thought about your own organization is likely to lead to a better result. As Pfeffer and Sutton (2006) argue, companies need evidence-based management. Simply trying to replicate the visible and relatively simple aspects of what another organization is doing will not be successful. So if the CEO calls, acknowledge his interest in recognition; tell him it is a great idea and agree that improving recognition is likely to be beneficial. But explain that as your organization is different from Big Co, you would like to look at what approach to recognition is likely to deliver best value for money.

You might also remember that like any other change, it works best from the top. So find the best way to start to get the CEO to recognize others – starting with his own reports. Recognition can be cascaded.

Programme usage

I do not recommend that you measure success simply by the number of recognition awards used. It may be a factor that you want to consider but ideally you need to get underneath this and look for changes in attitudes or behaviours. But monitoring the usage is sensible. If it drops off you may want to look at refreshing the programme. But do not set usage targets. If you do so you may well damage the whole programme by encouraging nominations or awards that are not appropriate.

Haringey Council monitored the usage of their customer programme and saw a steady increase over the three years after it was introduced. Prudential also monitor the usage and give the information to their HR business partners within the divisions but just as one of the many pieces of information available to them. They use this in their discussions about what is happening in the business, not to whip up support of the programme.

Take your time

Success outcomes need to be considered over time. If you want to increase the impact of recognition in your organization, it will take some time to show. So consider defining success outcomes over one, two and three years. Be very cautious about simply using those things that are easy to measure, like the usage rate. This might be a useful indicator and certainly if your aim is to encourage a lot of opportunities for people to be recognized, then high usage may be a positive indicator. More interesting is to look at the trend of usage over time. If it starts to drop, it may mean that the programme needs refreshing. I suggest using an employee engagement survey that includes a measure of recognition.

Employee and customer surveys

Attitude/satisfaction surveys of employees and customers can be both a stimulus to introduce a recognition programme and the means of identifying its success.

Here is an interesting example from a non-case study company, RSA, the global insurance group. RSA have used an annual engagement survey for some years. In 2004 their recognition score from the survey was only 41 per cent favourable. RSA identified the relatively low recognition score as one they wanted to improve as part of their aim of increasing the level of employee engagement. With this in mind, RSA introduced a number of programmes and changes over the next few years to help drive an improvement in the recognition score. The highlights include introducing the following:

- Greater rigour into the performance management process, including SMART goals and greater differentiation on performance. This process linked to a revised reward strategy where they rewarded their top performers more generously through bonus and long-term incentives (share options that vest after three years). They also rolled out a robust HR validation process that took place twice a year before performance appraisals happen. This was to increase rigour and fairness and also to ensure that they had the right spread of performance ratings in line with high-performing organizations.

- Employee recognition shop – an online shop where all people leaders could go to buy a broad range of gifts and vouchers with which to reward and thank their team members. All people leaders were given a budget to spend.

- Thank-you branded cards, which were given to leaders so they could say thank you to their team members when they had gone the extra mile.

- Group-wide recognition scheme called 'Platinum club', which is run in each region. Employees get to nominate who they think has done a great job in line with the brand beliefs, and submit an entry form. A panel of judges decides on a list of finalists and takes into account people's performance ratings. Finalists are then invited to a five-star awards evening where a number of them are selected as winners. The winners then go on an amazing holiday together with their partners. This generates massive uptake each year and employee feedback continues to be very positive. RSA continued with this programme even during the more turbulent economic times. Finalists and winners have commented that this says something about the kind of business RSA is.

By 2007 RSA saw that the recognition score had moved up by a remarkable 27 per cent to 68 per cent favourable. In 2008 RSA changed to a new survey partner, Gallup, which sets a higher bar of 'I have received recognition in the last seven days.' RSA have moved positively on the recognition score since they started working with Gallup.

Changes over time

A FTSE 100 business saw what they believed to be a low level of recognition in the organization as perceived by their people through the annual engagement survey. As a result of this, they introduced five different recognition programmes, from the very informal to the formal corporate programmes to help improve the recognition culture in the business. Over five years they saw a gradual improvement in how people felt about the way they were recognized. In the fifth year after the changes had been made, the attitude survey reported that 82 per cent of people agreed that 'I am thanked by my manager for a job well done.' And 73 per cent agreed that 'I am satisfied with the recognition I receive from my manager for doing my job well.' These are both high positive scores and significant improvements over the levels they started at five years before.

If you establish a baseline level of how people feel about recognition from an engagement survey, you could target an improvement of the 'recognition score' after introducing a range of recognition-related interventions. This can be a sensible target to help assess the impact of these interventions. Exit or termination interviews are also a valuable source of information. Again, they may be used to help identify if there is a lack of recognition in the organization as well as helping to track changes post implementation.

What sort of recognition programme?

As I showed in Chapter 4, there are broadly three levels of recognition plan:

- day to day;
- informal;
- formal.

Where you start will depend on what you want to achieve. But I suggest that the easiest place to start and the one that will make most impact is with the day to day. You may wish to issue simple guidelines to managers to help them understand what this is about. Recognition needs to be about a cultural change, so also build recognition behaviours into your management learning and development.

Review what's there

Even if no recognition programmes have been formally implemented, it is common to find a range of existing recognition practices within the organization. This is particularly likely in a decentralized organization. You can often find pockets of activity, normally driven by a local manager who has introduced simple ways to recognize people. Before developing a completely new recognition programme, try to find out what people are already doing. There is a danger that you can replace effective local arrangements with a centrally driven recognition programme that is nowhere near as effective. You really need to question your motives if this is a direction you are tempted to go down. If you want to expand the recognition that is going on in the organization, then it is better to work with the managers who already seem to be doing good work in recognizing their people to develop a programme that can be used more widely.

When British Airways were looking to introduce recognition programmes, they found that some departments already had their own recognition programmes operating at varying levels of success and funded within their budgets. These programmes were each different and were owned by each department. There was no attempt by HR to stifle these local initiatives or take them over as centralized processes; rather they were incorporated in broad reference in the management guide.

Sky and Standard Chartered take a decentralized approach and encourage local recognition programmes and approaches. Prudential, on the other hand, chose to replace the different individual recognition programmes with their new plan that went across the organization.

Maximizing effectiveness

Designing and developing effective communications and publicity are critical to maximize the effectiveness of recognition programmes. This needs to be considered from a number of angles:

- Publicize/launch the whole programme. If it is designed just to encourage managers to thank and recognize people fairly informally, then you may not wish to communicate the scheme outside the manager group. Otherwise, as Gryna (1992) advocates, publicity is the key to launching and continuing a successful recognition programme. One way to begin this process is to encourage employee participation when designing the programme. The longer the same programme is used, the more difficult it is to keep continued employee enthusiasm, therefore significant emphasis must be placed on continued publicity.
- Materials used to launch the programme need to be high quality and look professional. The quality of the material can be important to the success of the scheme. It reflects the sort of quality associated with customers: the message being that employees are important and we have gone to as much care with this scheme as if it had been something for our external customers.
- Brief managers or others involved – the programme(s) may need to be built into, for example, management training and induction programmes as many of the case study organizations do. If you want people to start to recognize others, you will need to give guidance to them on how best to do so.
- Publicize formal programme winners so that what they have done can be shared throughout the organization as role models. The choice of media will depend on your normal channels, but company newspapers or intranet are common. Real stories of what real people have done can be very positive and something that colleagues can identify with.

Name of the programme

Day-to-day recognition should not be thought of as a programme that needs a name. But informal and formal programmes are usually branded.

You may already have a theme into which the recognition programme name will fit. If it is being introduced to support the corporate values, you may wish to think of a name that reflects the values approach. Some organizations use a name that reflects something of their corporate brand. If you introduce a decentralized local recognition approach, like Sky, you will want the names used to be determined by the local group. Sky has different programmes with names devised locally that directly or indirectly reflect what the local group does.

Names often reflect something of the ethos of the programme, such as KPMG's 'Encore!' and 3's 'Round of applause', or Prudential's simple 'Recognition'. If you have a series of programmes, you may wish to link their names as Edexcel has done with their three programmes, each of which is prefixed with 'Star'.

Building a series of programmes over time

Formal programme

When people think of recognition programmes, it is often the more formal employee of the year type of schemes that come to mind. Some organizations' reaction to a lack of thanks and appreciation is to bureaucratize this into an HR-driven corporate programme. It is fairly easy to design a single high-profile company-wide scheme that will allow the CEO to mouth some platitudes on people being our greatest asset at a corporate event. But does it help to change the culture and will it have a positive impact?

A rules-driven recognition programme is more likely to constrain rather than encourage true recognition. Herzberg believed that recognition of individual achievement is unlikely to flourish in a bureaucratic situation. The framework of rules and regulations may constrain the opportunity to display individual achievement as well as the opportunity to recognize it.

Informal programme

The more informal local approach, which people can more easily relate to and is open ended, is likely to be more effective than the large corporate event, particularly as with the latter there are normally a pre-stated number of 'winners' permissible. So the place to start is not with the top-down corporate programme but with the informal local programmes. Try to drive the genuine recognition of people in an immediate, spontaneous way through providing guidance and access to some suitable awards. Comet have a series of programmes and provide their managers with a 'Recognition toolkit' to help them find ways to recognize their people effectively.

A new informal programme may need to 'bed down' over a year or so before any additional programmes could be introduced. But talk to line managers and others in the organization and review engagement survey results. Review what is going on and see if there is a place for a more formal arrangement in addition to the informal programme.

Additional programmes

You may wish to add a second level of programme that has as its starting point all of those people recognized informally. As an alternative, depending on the informality of the local programme, you may wish to add a slightly higher-value recognition opportunity that requires some sort of written statement about the action deserving recognition, etc. This may go to a central point or local coordinator to note or authorize a higher-value award.

From the informal programme, you can input nominations to a more formal recognition event to be held quarterly, half yearly or annually. I favour the shorter periods, as with an annual formal recognition programme it can be a very long time between the action and the formal award. You will need to consider carefully the level of profile, celebration and publicity of this more formal recognition event. Also study carefully the section on winners and losers in Chapter 4.

My survey found that the 61 participating major UK companies with recognition programmes had 116 programmes between them. This is illustrated in Table 5.2. The survey also showed that the majority (65 per cent) of recognition programmes operated are at the informal end of the continuum.

TABLE 5.2   Survey of 61 major UK companies with 116 recognition programmes

Number of recognition programmes	Percentage of organizations with that number of programmes
1	59
2	16
3	13
4	0
5	10
6	2

Where there is more than one programme, they are often designed for different groups such as sales or customer services rather than corporate functions. Also, some companies design programmes just for team rather than individual nomination. These are frequently very similar to the individual programme. Where there are a number of programmes that are common across the company, they are usually linked so that people recognized informally may go on as nominees to a more formal programme.

Using third-party providers

Introduction

Whether or not you use an external third-party provider and what, if any, support and services you might want from them will depend on your aims. This is a very important point. Start with your aims and what you want to achieve in the short and longer term. If you start with an external provider, you are in danger of buying their system and fitting it to your organization rather than the other way round. There are many excellent providers with some great systems, but be critical and look for some strong evidence of what impact they can make. Some of the case study organizations (3, KPMG, Prudential, Sky) use a third-party online system to manage their programmes in some way. These may provide points that can be converted to prizes or a system to easily source vouchers or other awards.

Types of third-party provider

In addition to independent consultancy expertise to help you develop an approach that may work best for you, there are broadly two types of third-party provider you might want to consider:

- providers who can source gifts and awards that can be used in different ways within the organization. For example, managers have access to a third-party website where they can order gifts and awards for their people. If you want a manager-led non-cash recognition or incentive scheme, you are more likely to consider this. I believe that there are many advantages in using this sort of third-party organization to provide gifts and awards. The main advantages are:

  - *Flexibility.* A single provider can be used, but they should be able to offer a wide range of gifts and also support different decentralized approaches to recognition.
  - *Time effective.* With a simple system a manager can access a suitable gift without spending their own time or the time of others to go out and buy something.
  - *Ease.* Because a system is available, managers are more likely to use it rather than delay.
  - *Fast.* A good third party can deliver a gift quickly to the manager or the individual.
  - *Control and tax.* Accessing gifts through a third-party system should ensure you capture data to ensure tax compliance.

- Providers of recognition and incentive systems that provide a recognition infrastructure, typically on-line using points, as well as sourcing gifts.

If you want a common organization-wide scheme where people can recognize each other, the latter approach is worth considering. But such an approach would need to follow your recognition strategy. I give an example in Chapter 8 of one UK company operating in a homogeneous business where this sort of third-party points-based arrangement was very effective.

There are a number of providers who claim to be able to operate such a system globally. If you want to consider this route, check carefully that the local tax issues are covered. Also ensure that the nature of the gifts or vouchers is appropriate and available in every country. I know of two companies who found that the vouchers provided by their global third-party partner could not be used in some of the countries. I would caution about following this global approach just for the sake of neatness and consistency. I am not sure that these criteria are best applied to recognition, which by its very nature may be applied differently from place to place and manager to manager.

Cost base

You need to understand exactly how providers generate income. It may be on fees as well, but will be to some extent normally from margins on the goods and services they supply. So the greater the volume and the higher the value, the greater their income. This is a perfectly reasonable business model, but you need to bear it in mind as inevitably this could influence their advice, in particular as to the value of gifts and awards for recognition programmes.

For a recognition programme you do not need such high-value items as you would with an incentive programme. As I have said before, recognition is primarily about the behaviour and the message, whereas an incentive is about the aim and the value. With an incentive programme you need to ensure that whatever is on offer is sufficiently valued by the potential recipients so that it will act as an incentive. For a recognition programme, lower-value non-cash awards will be more appropriate so as not to undermine the recognition message. So you will need to spend more per head on an incentive than on a recognition programme.

Why use a third-party provider

Particularly larger organizations look to outsource their internal recognition programme to third-party suppliers who can act as a one-stop shop for all of their non-cash incentive and recognition requirements. The reasons for using a third-party provider are:

- to gain greater control over recognition spending;
- to produce fully auditable management information;
- to capture data to ensure tax compliance;
- to reduce the internal administration required to run a scheme of this kind.

What to look for

Here are some of the things to look for in a third-party provider:

- *Appropriate gift range*. The third-party provider should have a suitable gift range available to cover different divisions within the organization, and also different groups of employees, interests and cultures. Core traditional gifts, such as flowers, hampers, wine, champagne, chocolates, may need to be complemented with some experience vouchers, hotel breaks, pamper days, theatre breaks, etc. You may also need a supplier that has access to higher-value items, such as electronics, jewellery and luxury pamper products. The provider would ideally have access to a range of high-street vouchers.
- *Quality*. It is generally better if the third-party company does not outsource many gifts to other providers. Ideally, core gifts should be sent out from one central location where the third-party company can control the quality of the gifts as they go out. If a poor-quality gift is sent out, this can have a negative reaction by the recipient.

- *Quick delivery.* The third-party provider needs to offer quick delivery, ideally next day. The faster the gift gets to the recipient, the stronger the link between behaviour and recognition.
- *White label website.* For organizations where employees have access to the internet, the easiest recognition scheme delivery mechanism is a bespoke website. This should be fully branded and should have little or no mention of the third-party provider. The website should have a wide range of functionality including several different security settings, options like authorized IP address lock-down, delivery to pre-stored addresses only, and role-driven access to different levels of gifts. The website should have the capability of identifying the user from login and displaying several different sub-brands, if relevant for different divisions. Live reporting should also be available with several different levels of access relating to the preset employee role of the individual accessing them.
- *Paper-based scheme.* The third-party provider should be able to offer a paper-based scheme for organizations where some of their employees do not have internet access: for example, field engineers. For these cases a bespoke white label paper brochure is likely to be the most effective.
- *Management information (MI).* This is a crucial element in selecting the appropriate third-party provider. MI gives organizations control over their spending and eliminates leakage. Live web-based reporting is a major benefit but the ability to also offer extensive MI for paper-based schemes is important. Ideally MI should be fully auditable and also provide suitable reports to cover tax issues.
- *Bespoke packaging.* The ability to offer bespoke branded packaging may be important as it can enhance the perceived value of the gift. Gifts that are wrapped in bespoke wrapping may be seen as more personal.
- *Own voucher/points system.* Depending on the sort of programme you want, you may need a provider who has a system offering suitable vouchers/points that can be redeemed against different products, allowing the recipient an appropriate choice.

- *Customer service.* The third-party provider should have their own customer service department to deal with any issue that occurs with regard to the gift or the delivery of the gift, as this prevents issues escalating back to the organization.
- *Account management.* The third-party provider should provide a single point of contact who fully understands their account and their requirements.
- *Costs.* There are third-party suppliers in the market who will offer a quality of service and charge for nothing but the gift and the delivery of the gift. So the organization should not have to pay any set-up fee, management fee, branded wrapping fee or website building fee (if they require standard functionality). However, depending on the volume, it may be more appropriate to pay a fee. You will need to check all the costs carefully, including a basket of common items, to compare the forecast overall costs of providers who do and do not charge fees or other set-up costs.

Regular review

Even if a recognition programme is seen to be effective, like any other HR programme, to keep it effective, it needs to be periodically reviewed. You should keep monitoring the schemes and have a formal review every two or three years. Indicators of a need to review a recognition programme are:

- loss of excitement so that no one talks about the programme;
- reducing participation;
- fewer people turn up at presentations;
- complaints about the winners.

The programme can be rejuvenated in many different ways such as:

- celebrating, say the 500th award;
- changing the choice of awards;
- adding a special category such as team award;
- changing the group who may select nominees for a corporate award;

- linking the programme to other initiatives such as suggestion schemes.

KEY JOBS TO DO

- Review the aims of your recognition strategy.
- Consider introducing or amending your engagement survey to capture recognition.
- Review what recognition activities already exist around your organization.
- Consider using a third-party provider to support your programmes.
- Review and refresh your recognition programmes if you have not done so within the last two years.

Chapter six
The cost and effectiveness of recognition programmes

"Recognition is so easy to do and so inexpensive to distribute that there is simply no excuse for not doing it. ROSABETH MOSS KANTER

THIS CHAPTER COVERS

- measuring the effectiveness of recognition programmes;
- cost and budgeting for recognition;
- tax and national insurance.

Measuring the effectiveness of recognition programmes

Anecdotal or measurement

There is plenty of anecdotal evidence of the cost effectiveness of re-cognition programmes. For example, Boyle (1995) says, 'When we say "Thank you" to our employees, productivity goes through the ceiling.

Recognition from within the organization is more important to employees than money.' Boyle argues that a recognition programme that rewards mean performance reduces the dips in performance while slowly and incrementally building up the mean of performance.

Of respondents to my survey, 74 per cent agreed with the statement that 'The recognition programmes that we operate are very good value for money.'

La Motta (1995) found that only about one-third of companies could answer a question on how effective their recognition programmes were. Even those answers were often vague. Friedson (1985) suggests that although the benefits of recognition programmes may be difficult to quantify, so too are the deficits that result from the lack of this type of recognition. Even if the direct effect of recognition programmes cannot easily be measured, they should still be able to send important messages about the value the organization places on a particular behaviour (Flannery et al, 1996). To that extent these programmes can be effective in reinforcing corporate values and making the belief system more tangible.

Typical ways to measure

A 2008 World at Work survey of US organizations found that 36 per cent of organizations did not measure the success of their recognition programmes. Of those that did, the measures they used were as shown in Table 6.1.

TABLE 6.1 Success measures used by US organizations

	%
Employee satisfaction surveys	43
Number of nominations	28
Turnover	26
Usage rates and/or participation rates	25
Productivity	15
Customer surveys	15
Return on investment	8

A 2009 survey of US and non-US companies found that 24 per cent did not measure the impact of recognition (or reward) programmes (The Ascent Group). Those that did measure effectiveness used a number of methods as shown in Table 6.2.

TABLE 6.2   Methods used for measuring reward and recognition programme success

	%
Feedback/focus groups	57
Employee surveys	53
Review performance results	53
Review budget/payout	30

A number of the case study organizations use employee engagement surveys to monitor the effectiveness of their recognition programmes. In some cases they have regularly reviewed the effectiveness of their programmes and relaunched them or made other changes based on feedback.

External comparison

You may well be able to compare your recognition scores from an engagement survey with external comparator data, if you use a major engagement survey such as the Gallup Q12. Or there may be other sources of external comparison against which you can benchmark your organization's performance. For example, the points-based recognition programme in the USA, the 100 Club mentioned in Chapter 3, had a very positive effect on the suggestion scheme compared with companies operating a suggestion scheme without the recognition programme (Boyle, 1995). This is shown in Table 6.3. The US companies with a 100 Club operating had a considerably greater participation rate in the suggestion schemes and a higher adoption rate of suggestions.

TABLE 6.3 Suggestion plan comparison; per 100 employees per annum

	US companies	US companies with 100 Club
Number of suggestions	13	168
Number of employees submitting	8	22
Number of adoptions	3	90
Adoption rate	24%	54%

Employee relations

The introduction of a recognition programme can have a positive effect on employee relations. It may even act as a catalyst to change the behaviour and attitudes present. For example, a strongly unionized plant in the US had a formal negotiated pay agreement. However, a recognition programme was introduced using a joint management and employee group to work on the plan. On implementation there was a very high degree of scepticism from the unionized employees, who had only ever seen gains through 'hard-fought negotiations'. They were suspicious of a hidden agenda. But over time, the recognition of things being done that were simply what was expected was both accepted and showed considerable improvements in the key areas being focused on.

Whereas the management may have had considerable difficulties in trying to make such changes through a negotiated pay-based mechanism, by introducing a non-cash recognition programme outside the pay arena, and ensuring it was entirely in addition to other elements, considerable benefits were gained. It was claimed that following the introduction of the programme productivity increases of 14.5 per cent were made, worth over $5.2 million (£3.5 million) (Boyle, 1995). These benefits were seen to be both directly from the recognition programme and more indirectly from the improvement in labour management relations that the programme engendered.

When you get it right

Las Vegas-based hotel and casino group MGM Grand sees recognition as a major part of its culture (*Workspan*, August 2008). They have a series of recognition programmes and have seen a number of key metrics improve since they introduced them. They believe that their employee recognition programme has increased revenue and improved employee morale and retention. They say, 'At MGM Grand, we have found that recognition is important business. It is clear that effective recognition, in all its forms, strongly enhances morale and ultimately increases productivity in the workplace. When you have an effective employee recognition program, that makes for good business, and everybody wins.'

The O.C. Tanner Company commissioned research on 26,000 employees in 31 healthcare organizations in the USA by an independent market research company, The Jackson Organization (Gostick and Elton, 2007). Respondents were asked to state their level of agreement to the statement, 'My organization recognizes excellence.' The responses were averaged and grouped into four quartiles, the most positive responses being the fourth quartile and the least positive the first quartile. They found a positive correlation between the mean scores to this question and return on equity (ROE), return on assets (ROA) and operating margin as shown in Table 6.4. Each of these three measures can be key in looking at the financial health of an organization. ROE is the earnings in the financial year divided by the average shareholder's equity for the same year. ROA is the earnings divided by the total assets. Operating margin is the ratio of operating income to sales.

TABLE 6.4 Quartile analysis: 'My organization recognizes excellence'

	Least positive %	%	Most positive %	%
Quartile	1	2	3	4
Return on equity	2.4	3.6	5.3	8.7
Return on assets	1.7	2.1	3.6	6.1
Operating margin	1.0	2.4	4.1	6.6

The Jackson Organization said, 'Up until this study, the link between recognition and financial performance was largely anecdotal. Recognition was considered by some to be an emotional afterthought, while those who believed that effective recognition would drive results had no hard data to prove it. This study took recognition results from myth to reality – from the soft side of business to a proven business essential.'

The cost of recognition

Introduction

The bottom line with recognition is that it costs very little, particularly compared with the impact it can have. Ed Lawler says that 'People respond to something that costs little or nothing, and that something is called recognition.' But it may still make sense to try to understand the costs. However, a survey of over 100 companies in the USA found that only four companies could give any indication of the costs of their programmes (La Motta, 1995). With a very decentralized approach with low-value non-cash awards, an organization might decide that it is not worth trying to capture the costs centrally.

Budgets

A 1992 survey of 67 US companies (Conference Board Inc, 1992) found that the budgets for non-cash award programmes varied by company size as shown in Table 6.5.

TABLE 6.5 Budgets for non-cash award programmes

Number of employees	Median budget (updated to 2009)
<4,000	$45,000 (£30,000)
4,000–10,000	$75,000 (£50,000)
10,000–30,000	$300,000 (£200,000)
>30,000	$950,000 (£633,000)

A significant difference between pay systems and recognition is cost. Whereas pay can be up to 70 per cent of an organization's costs, recognition programmes are relatively cheap to run. Friedson (1985) suggests that as a rule of thumb corporations with award programmes should budget between 0.5 per cent to 1.0 per cent of payroll to fund them, although he also says that much of that money is often left unspent.

A very informal recognition programme can cost almost nothing. Maynard (1997) quotes the CEO of a US food company, which operates a number of recognition award programmes, who says that 'though there may be economic restraints on what we pay them, there are no restraints on the recognition we give them'.

The average cost of recognition programmes for the UK companies in my survey was less than 0.5 per cent of payroll.

What should you budget for recognition programmes?

Central or local budgets

Even where no corporately sponsored programmes exist it is common to find pockets of good recognition practice within organizations. Managers who understand the value of such an approach often find a way to fund some informal local recognition, such as sending a successful team out to dinner or presenting someone with a case of wine. They will find some money within their existing budget. It is important that the introduction of a broader programme does not stifle these initiatives – rather it should learn from and capitalize on them. One approach is to ensure that every manager has a small budget for local recognition awards. This is the approach that Harvey-Jones (1994) advocated: 'every manager should have a small "float" to enable him to produce such forms of recognition in whatever seems the most appropriate way'.

Where an informal non-cash award programme is being established, it may be budgeted for within each department or centrally. There is an argument for a central budget initially to get it off the ground. Also, there may be a significant over- or underspend, as you cannot limit recognition to a quota. Inevitably some departments will use a recognition programme more than others. A local budget can lead to managing strictly to the budget so that recognition is undertaken just to meet a quota or budget rather than there being a genuine desire to use the award effectively to recognize something great someone has done.

Creating a budget

Depending on the particular organization, a way to create some budget for non-cash recognition is simply to carve out a small amount from the cash bonus pot or pay review. Typically, the amount needed for recognition is trivial compared with these often substantial sums. Depending on the pay/bonus mix in the organization, you may find that less than 0.1 per cent of payroll or 0.25 per cent of bonuses would give enough for a recognition programme. And think of the potential leverage that you could get from this spend.

What elements to budget

If you are looking at a more formal recognition programme you will need to budget for things such as:

- initial publicity and launch materials – posters, guidelines, intranet;
- cost of the awards themselves;
- certificates or trophies;
- celebration events – catering, venue, invitations, etc;
- management time;
- tax and national insurance on awards.

Tax and national insurance

Introduction

This section covers the tax and payroll tax situation in the UK, but some of the underlying principles may apply in other jurisdictions. Certainly, anyone planning to introduce non-cash awards needs to check the position with the local tax authorities or take appropriate local professional advice.

A potential risk of local informal arrangements to provide employees with recognition awards is that any tax or national insurance contribution (NIC) liability is not correctly accounted for. It does happen that awards are given to employees on which tax and NIC are due but are just not accounted for. All organizations should take appropriate steps to ensure that they do capture this information. This is one reason for organizations to use a single provider to facilitate such gifts. The third-party organization will be able to provide the appropriate management information to ensure that the organization can then manage their risk by capturing all tax and NIC liabilities and settling them so as to remain compliant.

It is normal practice for the employer to settle any employee tax and NIC arising from a recognition award. It is therefore important to discuss this with your tax department or tax advisors early on. Whatever cost estimates or budget you set will need to take this cost into account. It is better to provide a lower-value gift and pay the tax than a higher-value one where the employee finds themselves paying tax they did not expect. The enthusiasm and goodwill generated from a non-cash award is immediately damaged, even destroyed, if the employee suddenly finds themselves taxed on the benefit. Some organizations have found people refuse to accept a gift on which they may have to pay tax. In these situations the message is generally 'If the tax I am going to have to pay is more valuable to me than the gift, that I can do without – so don't bother!'

Assuming that you follow my advice, then make sure that it is clear to any recipient that the organization will pay any tax due; they need not worry about it.

Taxation of non-cash awards

As a general principle, an employer should assume that any gift, award or vouchers given to an employee is subject to tax and NIC deductions. However, it may be that a gift may not be taxable if it is considered 'trivial', or may fall under another non-taxable category, which may change from time to time. Although HMRC use the term 'trivial' they do not define it as such. There are no set rules for determining the type of benefit that is trivial, and there is no set monetary limit below which benefits are deemed to be trivial in amount. HMRC expect employers to apply common sense and judgement both to the type and the amount of benefits that they consider to be trivial. But HMRC do give some guidance. They note that trivial benefits are often, but not always, perishable and/or consumable. HMRC do consider two categories, small gifts and seasonal gifts:

- Small gifts – such as an arrangement of flowers made in recognition of a particular event (eg an employee's marriage or birth of a child) and – importantly – that do not form part of any reward for the employee's services.
- Seasonal gifts – such as a turkey, an ordinary bottle of wine or a box of chocolates at Christmas.

When considering whether a trivial benefit should be ignored for practical purposes, bear the following factors in mind:

- the cost of the benefit provided to each employee, and not the overall cost to the employer of providing the benefit;
- the term 'trivial' should not be viewed relative to the level of an employee's income;
- the administrative and time cost (to you as employer and to HMRC) in handling the associated reporting requirements (forms P11D, and coding and self-assessment), in relation to the amounts of tax and NIC at stake.

Cash benefits, benefits with a money's worth and non-cash vouchers, however small in amount, should not be regarded as trivial.

It may be possible therefore to consider a gift of a bottle wine or a bunch of flowers or similar as part of a non-cash recognition scheme to be trivial and so not taxable. However, 'recognition' here needs to be event based rather than linked to a reward for services rendered. And if you move to a case of wine or a Christmas hamper, then it is almost certainly going to be subject to tax. The most common way for organizations to settle any tax due on items that are not accepted by HMRC as trivial is through a PAYE settlement agreement (PSA).

PAYE settlement agreement

A PSA is a voluntary arrangement on the part of the employer and can be used to include items that are minor, irregular or impractical to apply PAYE/NIC to, or apportion the value of a particular benefit. For practical purposes it may be that small cash and money's worth benefits can be included in a PSA. This can be a convenient way for employers to deal with the position on small (if not 'trivial') recognition awards without involving the individual employee. That said, it is important to tell the employee that this is your intention so that they are clear that they don't need to worry about the tax themselves. Your local inspector of taxes may agree a 'blended tax rate' to be used within your PSA based on the proportion of basic rate and higher-rate taxpayers in your population who receive non-cash awards. This would generally need to be reviewed annually. It is not going to be exact, but will be much simpler and easier to apply.

The PSA approach is likely to be preferable for awards to an organization's own employees. But employers can also enter into a special accounting arrangement for non-cash awards called a taxed award scheme (TAS). This arrangement can be used to account directly for tax on awards to their own or other people's employees, or both. However, unlike awards covered by PSAs, non-cash awards and the tax paid on them under TAS arrangements remain assessable on the employee. So the employee has to enter the grossed-up value of the award and the tax paid on it into their tax return. But normally no further tax is due from an employee, unless the provider has only entered into a basic-rate TAS and the recipient of the award is liable at the higher rate. But as it is not a good idea to leave the employee to pay tax, I recommend that TAS is only used if making an award to someone else's employee such as a contractor.

Suggestion schemes

HMRC allow some awards as part of a suggestion scheme to be exempt from tax and NIC. For an award to qualify for this exemption:

- The suggestion scheme must be open to all your employees – or to an entire group of employees, such as everyone based in a particular office.
- The suggestion leading to the award must relate to your business.
- The employee receiving the award couldn't reasonably be expected to have made the suggestion in the course of their normal duties of employment.
- The suggestion can't have been made at a meeting held for the purposes of proposing suggestions.
- The award must be either an 'encouragement award' or a 'financial benefit' award.

An encouragement award is an award made to an employee for a suggestion that has merit or that shows special effort on the employee's part. Encouragement awards are exempt from tax and NIC up to a small limit of (currently) £25 ($38).

A financial benefit award is an award made to an employee for a suggestion that meets the following three conditions:

- It relates to an improvement in efficiency or effectiveness.
- The organization must have decided to adopt the suggestion.
- The organization must reasonably expect the suggestion's implementation to lead to a financial benefit.

Financial benefit awards are exempt from tax and NIC up to the greater of the following limits, subject to an overall limit of (currently) £5,000 ($7,500):

- 50 per cent of the financial benefit you reasonably expect the suggestion to lead to in the first year following its adoption; or
- 10 per cent of the financial benefit you reasonably expect in the first five years following adoption.

If you make an encouragement award or financial benefit award up to the limits, then you have no reporting requirements and no tax or NIC to pay. If you make an award above the limits set, any excess counts as earnings, so must be put through PAYE.

Long service awards

There are also currently tax exemptions for long service awards, provided they fall within certain limits. The awards should be:

- in the form of a tangible article or shares in an employing company (or another company in a group of companies);
- for a minimum recognition period of service of 20 years;
- up to a maximum spend of £50 ($75) per year of service; and
- with a minimum 10-year break between awards.

So long as these four criteria are met, the service award is free of tax and does not need to be reported. Because these limits are fairly generous (£1,000 ($1,500) value at 20 years, and a further £500 ($750) value at 30 years), many companies restrict long service awards to these limits and so ensure there is no tax to pay. If a higher value is used than the £50 ($75) per year of service, then any excess over the limit is taxable.

Some organizations present awards at a celebratory event, so it is worth mentioning a final tax exemption. An annual function provided by the employer that is open to all employees (or at least all employees at a particular location) and where the average cost per head does not exceed £150 ($225) including VAT does not give rise to a tax charge. This exemption also applies where there is more than one function in the tax year provided the aggregate cost per head does not exceed £150 ($225).

This section on tax and NIC is a general guide only on the position in the UK and should not be relied upon as the legislation changes regularly. You are therefore strongly advised to take professional advice at the time. You may also find that the HMRC website will give you useful information. It is certainly a good first step.

KEY JOBS TO DO

- Consider appropriate measures of success.
- Review the budget.
- Review your tax compliance.
- Ensure you are capitalizing on tax exemptions.

Chapter seven
How do recognition programmes fit with HR?

> *Friendship which is bought with money and not with greatness and nobility of mind is paid for, but it does not last and it yields nothing.*
>
> NICCOLÒ MACHIAVELLI

THIS CHAPTER COVERS

- the links between recognition and reward;
- the links between recognition and performance management;
- the links between recognition and learning and development.

Introduction

It is the whole person who comes to work and it is the totality of work that affects people. So it is important to think how recognition programmes relate to other HR programmes and how the different programmes can work together. For example, what messages do the existing pay programmes carry? If there is a link to performance, how does it work? What style and elements of leadership are promoted in management development and training programmes?

Recognition and reward

What is the relationship?

The relationship between recognition and reward is complex. However, Juran (2003) explains it well:

- Rewards are salary increases, bonuses, and promotions keyed to job performance and usually conferred in private, primarily focusing on conduct of operations using performance appraisal or merit ratings.
- Recognition is typically non-financial and consists of 'ceremonial' actions taken to publicize meritorious performance.

Adrian Furnham believes that most people believe that extrinsic motivation (money, holidays, etc) are more important motivators than the intrinsic (interesting and worthwhile work and responsibility) (*Employee Benefits*, September 2008). But he argues that it is actually the other way round. Recognition is one factor that actively contributes to employees' intrinsic satisfaction with their job.

British Airways simply but effectively differentiates as follows:

- Reward is about pay or compensation.
- Incentives are about meeting targets.
- Recognition is about saying 'Thank you'.

Rosabeth Moss Kantor simplifies it even further by saying, 'Compensation is a right, recognition is a gift.'

What is the message?

Another significant way to think about the two is that recognition is all about the message. Any tangible gift or award is simply a small element of the thanks. The impact is in the thanks. But with pay it is usually quite the opposite. You have to pay people for them to work for you; you are obliged to pay employees. Whatever else they know about a potential job, the one absolute is the pay.

It is not common for an organization to think about the message they want pay or bonus to carry. This misses a lot of value. It might seem odd that an organization could spend up to 70 per cent of its costs on pay and yet spend little time ensuring people understand what it is about. We can carry over some of the elements of effective recognition – the messages – into pay. So financial reward can be a form of recognition, inasmuch as it can be used to tell people more than that they are just being paid to do a job. Tyson (1995) considers that there are strong symbolic overtones within organizational rewards. 'Monetary rewards may not motivate in the long term, but they certainly symbolize the value corporations attach to specific behaviours – for example rewarding long service, interpreted as loyalty, or rewarding performance above other attributes.' So although pay programmes can be contrasted with recognition, the effectiveness of pay can be improved if its underlying symbolic effect is considered. If you want to see what an organization truly values, look at what it actually pays for – not what it says.

Although Herzberg is always held up as saying that money is a hygiene factor, not a motivator, he also saw a connection between pay, recognition and achievement. 'Money thus earned as a direct reward for outstanding individual performance is a reinforcement of the motivators of recognition and achievement. It is not hygiene as is money given in across-the-board wage increases' (Herzberg, 1968).

Recognition or incentives?

Non-cash recognition programmes should be contrasted with incentive plans such as bonuses. Recognition programmes are not incentive plans. They seek to change behaviour by reinforcing positive actions – they do not do so by using the incentive of a carrot. An incentive plan carries the message 'You do that and I will give you this.' A recognition programme, on the other hand, seeks to reinforce the great things people are already doing.

Many managers in the USA and UK have deeply held assumptions about the role of incentive pay in motivation. This can be because money is the only 'currency' used by some organizations to thank people; giving the message that it is only cash that demonstrates your worth (Nelson, 1996). In other words, these managers promote a self-fulfilling prophecy so that employees learn to expect cash as the only true form of thanks. If a child is deprived of love by its parents but receives only toys, then although it may crave the love, it ends up demanding more toys – the currency that the parent uses. The parallel with reward and recognition is clear – what is really needed is genuine appreciation and understanding by managers of employees. However, as with children, toys are better than nothing at all (La Motta, 1995). Non-cash recognition programmes can help to shift the balance back to real thanks and appreciation and so complement the pay system.

In this book I argue that effective recognition can have a powerful effect and that non-cash awards can deliver more value than cash. However, some organizations do use cash as the tangible element of their recognition programme. This is usually because it is simple and easy to manage. But you do need to differentiate between recognition and reward. If you set up a recognition scheme that can deliver different amounts of cash, particularly if it is delivered through payroll, it can easily lead managers to use the scheme to top up a poor pay review. This simply derails the recognition scheme and delivers confusing and mixed messages.

Recognition and performance management

Performance management systems often underpin performance-related pay. The challenge lies in developing a system that allows the effective translation of performance into pay. A survey by William M Mercer, on companies' performance-related pay systems, found that 47 per cent of companies reported that their employees 'found the systems neither fair nor sensible', with 51 per cent saying that the performance management system provided little value to the company.

Annual review

A classic approach to performance management is to use some form of annual objectives-based system where performance is reviewed against the objectives set. However, objectives and performance criteria can be very difficult to set, in particular as organizations change rapidly and there may be no tangible outputs. The individual is often rewarded for achievement against so-called SMART objectives. However, the emphasis on measurability can lead to objectives being selected because they can easily be measured rather than because they add value. Recognition programmes, on the other hand, do not try to incentivize people to achieve specific objectives, but celebrate and reinforce the great things people do.

Most organizations also try to reflect not just the 'what' people have done but also the 'how' they have done it. Some, like Standard Chartered, have taken it as far as using two ratings for these two elements of performance. Others use some form of balanced business scorecard and competence frameworks. Recognition is often a bridge between these. We are recognizing the great things people do that almost always combine the 'what' and the 'how'.

Although a key value in an appraisal-driven performance management system is 'no surprises' (at the annual review, because there should have been constant feedback throughout the year), in reality this is rarely the case. The annual cycle of performance and pay review has little real emphasis as part of the process on line managers providing more regular feedback and recognition. A non-cash recognition programme can be designed to promote recognizing the positive things people do at any time throughout the year and so can sit alongside the performance management process. Where someone has received some kind of recognition award, it should be referred to in the performance management discussions. The case study organizations do not have a formal link between their recognition programmes and their formal performance management systems. But in most cases they consider it reasonable, and some actually encourage, that any recognition during the year should be brought into the formal review.

If recognition of people is an important value in the organization, then you would also expect that individual managers would have their performance in effectively recognizing people to be one of the factors considered in their own appraisal.

Some organizations that have a recognition scheme where anyone can nominate anyone else requires the line manager of the person being nominated or sometimes HR to confirm that there are no other issues that could compromise an award. If, for example, the individual is in the disciplinary or performance improvement process, it may be felt inappropriate for them to receive a recognition award. Some organizations, on the other hand, see the two issues as quite separate.

Promotion

Promotion may seem the most obvious point at which reward and recognition come together. A promotion may help meet the self-esteem needs through wider recognition. Promotion may bring further intrinsic reward to the extent that the new job offers greater challenge and opportunity. However, the motivational effect of promotion may only be sustained for a relatively short period, so although promotion may play a part, it is questionable as a key means to recognize and reward performance (Pitts, 1995). Even so, with flatter organizational structures and an increase in broadbanding – 20 per cent of companies have broadbanding and another 17 per cent will be introducing it (CBI/Hay, 1995) – the opportunity for the more conventional promotions are becoming more limited. Although recognition through a suitable programme should not be a substitute for promotion and development, it can provide many more opportunities to recognize people in less formal but still significant and valued ways.

Recognition and learning and development

Where should it fit?

Recognition is an issue, like performance management, that does not fit neatly within either the reward function or the learning and development function. It really sits somewhere in between them. But rather like performance management, where the organization chooses to place recognition will dictate the emphasis that is given to it. Typically, recognition sits within reward. But I suggest that Figure 7.1 represents more realistically what the relationship ought to be between the reward and the learning and development teams and recognition and non-cash awards.

FIGURE 7.1   Where recognition fits

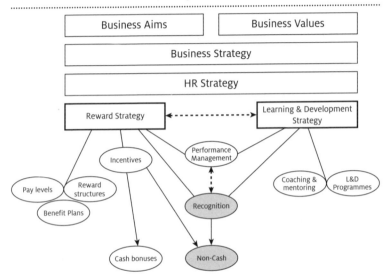

Herzberg (1959) saw that for a job to provide satisfaction there must be opportunity for achievement, which should also provide a learning opportunity. Recognition of achievement becomes the reinforcement necessary for learning, and is a key part of the feedback loop.

Non-cash recognition programmes are often introduced to help change behaviour in the management of people and the interaction of people in an organization; they may be part of a larger cultural change programme. In particular, organizations like Prudential have used recognition to help reinforce and embed values. A recognition programme can be particularly valuable to help people understand what a certain value actually means. By publicizing the great things people have done within any value helps bring the value to life so others may say, 'Ah, so that's what it is.'

Recognition needs to be defined in terms that the organization will understand and find useful and then should form part of a greater whole, not just stand on its own as the recognition programme. If one of the organization's values is to recognize people, then this needs to be reinforced not only through the non-cash recognition programme itself but in the training and development of the people who will operate it. So the value and impact of a recognition programme will be enhanced by ensuring that recognition is covered within your management learning and development programmes. Recognition can also be an important element of coaching and giving effective feedback.

Case study organizations 3, Comet, Edexcel, KPMG and Standard Chartered all cover recognition in one way or another within their management training programmes and in induction 'for new employees. Comet emphasize the need for management briefing and guidance with, for example, their 'manager recognition toolkit'. Standard Chartered have recognition as just one of the elements in their comprehensive management programmes, in particular emphasizing coaching discussions.

Development and training should help drive the same message of the importance and role of recognition in the motivation and management of people. Recognition programmes and training and development need to reinforce similar behaviours in a consistent and coherent way.

Role of HR and line management

The relative roles of HR and line management in recognition will depend on the way in which they work together on existing people-related issues. Typically, although HR will develop the recognition programmes in conjunction with line management, the programme will be used by the line. Recognition needs to be the sort of programme that is owned by the line managers. If it becomes seen as another HR project, then it is unlikely to be successful. It is therefore important that HR people work with the line managers to develop the programme, getting buy-in as they do so. As we have seen earlier, a centrally over-managed bureaucratic recognition programme is unlikely to deliver the value expected for the cost.

KEY JOBS TO DO

- Review the messages carried by the recognition programme and the links with reward, performance management and learning and development.
- Consider how you can improve the impact of reward by bringing to it some of the underlying aspects of recognition.
- Ensure the links are clear and build strategy and communications reflecting the desired links.

Chapter eight
Using non-cash as an incentive

> *Everything that can be counted does not necessarily count; everything that counts cannot necessarily be counted.* ALBERT EINSTEIN

THIS CHAPTER COVERS

- potential dangers in using financial incentives;
- motivation theories that underpin incentives;
- impact of time span on incentives;
- types of non-cash for incentives.

Introduction

Assumptions on cash incentives

Before I say anything else about incentives, I want to raise a fundamental point on the underlying assumptions about them. While incentives are considered by many managers as the most effective form of motivation, I hope I have so far in this book suggested that there are many ways to approach this. Incentives are clearly an extrinsic motivator and can lead to unintended consequences. There is always the danger of destroying some intrinsic motivation by putting a price on it through cash.

Professor Adrian Furnham tells the story of the writer who was disturbed by children playing in the park right by his office window. His solution was to go out and say to the children how much he enjoyed them playing there and gave them £1 each. He did this for a couple more days, but on the next day he told them that he was not going to pay them any more. Their reaction was that in that case they were going to play somewhere else.

In the USA the views on incentives are more deeply held than in other parts of the world:

> ...many managers in the USA and the UK – but not, incidentally, in continental Europe or Japan – have deeply held assumptions about the role of incentive pay in motivation. These assumptions lead them to engage compensation consultants in answering the wrong question: How should we design the incentive system in order to obtain the desired behaviour? The important question is: What role, if any, should incentive compensation play? ... Assumptions about incentive compensation have led many managers to expect incentives to solve organizational problems, when there are actually deeper underlying reasons for those problems.
>
> (Kerr, 1997)

The negative impact of financial incentives

There is evidence suggesting that financial incentives may not add value, but rather in some circumstances can actually have a negative impact. Sam Glucksberg, who is now at Princeton University, conducted an experiment into the effect of financial incentives as a motivator. Glucksberg took groups of participants and told them that he was going to time them to see how quickly they could solve a particular problem (the candle problem – to attach a candle to the wall without it dripping wax on the floor, given a candle, a box of tacks and some matches).

He divided the participants into two groups. He told one group that he was going to time them to determine how long it typically took people to solve this type of problem.

He offered the second group $5 (£3.30) if they were in the 25 per cent that solved the problem the fastest. In addition, the person who was the fastest of all would get $20.00 (£13.00).

It took the second group, that was offered the cash incentive, three and a half minutes longer, on average, to solve the problem than it took the first group.

Glucksberg repeated the experiment, except this time he presented not a box with tacks in it, but an empty box with the tacks on the table beside it. In other words, he made the problem easier because once the box was not being used as a container, less mental flexibility was needed to assign a different function to it. This time, the group that was being incentivized finished the task a lot faster than the other group.

The conclusion that may be drawn from these findings is that extrinsic rewards may work well for tasks with a simple set of rules and a clear aim. But rewards may narrow our focus and concentrate the mind. But for the real candle problem – the one with the thumb tacks in the box – you don't want tunnel vision; you want to be able to see what is on the periphery: you want to be looking around; you want to expand your possibilities. Dan Pink, in a talk titled 'The surprising side of motivation', concludes that 'As long as the task involved only mechanical skill, bonuses worked as they would be expected: the higher the pay, the better the performance. But once the task called for even rudimentary cognitive skill, a larger reward led to poorer performance.'

Alfie Kohn, a well-known critic of financial incentives, believes that 'Incentives, a version of what psychologists call extrinsic motivators, do not alter the attitudes that underlie our behaviours. They do not create an enduring commitment to any value or action. Rather, incentives merely – and temporarily – change what we do' (Kohn, 1993).

Even if you support using financial incentives, you need to take account of the potential cumulative effect they may have. Recipients of incentive schemes may well adjust their efforts to optimize the return they get via the incentive. To increase job performance you will need to offer new incentives (Human Capital Institute, 2009).

Conclusion

We need to at least question our assumptions about the effect of financial incentives. In isolation and applied inappropriately they may actually cause damage. But they can be positioned as part of a whole culture including recognition. But the truth remains that, if you want someone to do a good job, give them a good job to do.

Most of this book has been about using recognition to help motivate and engage people, often supported by non-cash awards. Recognition is about celebrating success and 'catching people doing something right'. It is not about predetermined targets or goals. But using non-cash reward can be more effective than cash as part of an incentive programme that is focused on getting people to achieve specific outcomes. The four reasons why non-cash scores over cash covered in Chapter 1 hold good whether for recognition or incentive:

- differentiation;
- memory value;
- perceived value;
- personal.

Before looking at how these might be applied as incentives it is worth considering the motivation theories that underpin some of this.

Motivation theories

There are two motivation theories that I think are most relevant: expectancy theory and one that was mentioned earlier, reinforcement theory.

Expectancy theory

The key theory behind incentives is Vroom's expectancy theory (1964), which says that the strength of any motivation will vary according to:

- the desires for a particular outcome;
- the expectancy that action will lead to the outcome;
- the likelihood that the goal can be achieved.

It is the consequences of attaining a goal that is significant rather than the intrinsic value of the goal itself. The theory is based on a rational cognitive approach, which assumes that a person will, in effect, weigh up the value to them of an outcome in terms of its consequences as well as the likelihood of it happening. So according to the theory people will pursue that level of performance that they believe will maximize their overall best interest. This would then predict that a reward given that was not contingent on behaviour, or was not expected to be contingent, would have no effect on the choices that an individual makes.

Social reinforcement

Social reinforcement is the reward that comes from acknowledgement from others for a job well done or achieving a particular level of success. Maslow talked about the motivator of the esteem of others. Clearly, it requires others to know of the success to enable them to acknowledge it.

These two theories can help us understand how non-cash reward can be effective as incentives.

My first proper job was with a direct selling life assurance company. I joined as a graduate trainee in 1975 and soon moved to work in training and development and then compensation. The sales people were on commission only, with no salary – clearly an environment with a very direct cash-based incentive reward strategy: if they did not sell, they did not eat. But not so. In addition to the cash commission, the company employed a whole range of non-cash awards, prizes and incentives. There was the million dollar round table, the chairman's club, the regional awards and the annual conventions in luxury locations abroad. What all of these things did was to enable the successful salespeople to demonstrate their success in a way that cash alone could not. Achieving these different non-cash awards were all about getting recognition and esteem from others. There was a degree of exclusivity about the prizes. Only a relatively small number would achieve them and be feted by the executives of the company.

Case study company Comet have a series of recognition programmes and financial bonus arrangements. But they also use non-cash as part of the whole incentive arrangements. The two featured – Millionaires' Club and Store Manager of the Year – address Maslow's esteem need from others. Although Comet do not pay direct commission, people who are successful in either of these programmes may well have received additional cash bonuses, but through these programmes they receive the acknowledgement of their colleagues of their success. Comet also recognize their achievements by asking them to give sales tips to others. Not only does this leverage successful sales ideas around the business, from people who will be respected, but it also gives further social reinforcement to those who have been successful.

Money itself is often 'converted' to a tangible image to try to keep people focused even where non-cash incentives are little used. The sales manager may well sit down with the new salesperson and try to get them to talk about their personal goals and see a cash incentive in terms of meeting those goals. The goals may be the new house, the new second car, the ease of paying school fees, that exotic holiday, the mortgage paid off – whatever it is that the individual really wants.

Time span

Organizations often give annual bonuses based on measures such as the sales, profit, costs and individual and team performance in the year. An important consideration, however, is to think about the time span over which the individual being incentivized has an impact. Where the performance period is a year or more it is most common to give cash incentives and shares where available. It is also normal practice and quite sensible to give such a bonus after the end of the year. But it does not make sense to try to use a payment period out of line with a performance period. So if the impact of the action that you are looking to reinforce through an incentive is a week or a month, it is not effective to pay a bonus after the end of the year. Rather like recognition, a bonus should be paid as close as possible to the end of the period when the action took place.

I would also argue that non-cash incentives can work particularly well over shorter periods. So a prize of a bottle of champagne at the end of the day for the best achiever or a day off for the top three at the end of the month can be very effective.

Teams often work on time-limited projects. A non-cash incentive and some celebration for achieving the team goals within the time targeted can be more effective than individual cash awards.

Types of non-cash award

Desirable

A number of examples of types of non-cash awards are given in Chapter 4. But where you are using non-cash as part of an incentive it is critical to make it desirable. With a recognition programme, it is the recognition itself that is important – the associated tangible awards are generally secondary. But with an incentive scheme, the participants must want what you are offering – that is a key element of Vroom's theory.

Look particularly for luxury aspirational awards and prizes as incentives. Exclusivity or rarity may be key. It is not so much a case of 'keeping up with the Joneses' in terms of what they have, but doing something that the Joneses' have not done. The trophy value is particularly important. One of the most common used prizes is incentive travel.

Incentive travel

There are a number of reasons why incentive travel is popular:

- Regardless of who actually achieves the trip, travel is an ideal incentive as its very nature allows you to present it in different media as a very attractive desirable experience. Companies often put together a promotional film about the next trip and use DVDs or online media to promote the trip.
- It can be made exclusive – by arranging elements that can be done as a group and which an individual traveller simply could not arrange. It is an experience, not just a holiday. The travel can be arranged so that the participants are treated like VIPs, for

example, with no queues for checking in and baggage managed so that once they leave it they next see it in their hotel room.

- It is something that the individual's partner can enjoy and which can reinforce to them their partner's success.
- A particular trip can be arranged a few months after the end of the performance period when the individual is already in the next performance, typically a sales cycle. It can therefore continue to help motivate for the current performance, not just having incentivized for the last one.
- As a group event, the individuals can be made to feel more connected to the group of successful people and the organization. Networking within that environment can lead to direct business benefits.

The destination and type of incentive trip you decide on will be based on many factors, with the cost related to the benefit as vital. The popularity of destinations will change from time to time. The top five destinations from a 2009 poll by *Conference and Incentive Travel* magazine were:

1 Dubai
2 London
3 South Africa
4 Barcelona
5 New York/Las Vegas.

Incentive travel is at the top end of non-cash incentives. But a simple points-based programme can be very effective to integrate a number of different desired aims as discussed in the next section.

Integrated use of non-cash incentives

Introduction

Non-cash incentives can be used to encourage a whole number of different desired behaviours and targets. Whereas individual cash amounts would be small and potentially unattractive, using a non-cash points-type system allows people to accumulate value in a number of different ways to acquire a relatively high-perceived-value gift. This is well illustrated in the following example.

Programme outline

A retail pub chain introduced a non-cash incentive programme based on the potential achievement of a range of individual and team aims and behaviours. With an outside provider, HR developed a high-gloss gifts catalogue with an associated points accumulation system. This was aimed primarily at the more than 10,000 people working in the pubs and restaurants. In the catalogue, in addition to the pictures and descriptions of the large range of gifts, there were also clear explanations of what had to be done to obtain gifts and also some simple associated pointers of how to improve performance within each of these areas. There were a number of different ways in which people could accumulate points:

- if the unit within which they worked exceeded its budgeted turnover in the period;
- a score based on a quarterly assessment of customer service based on visits by a mystery visitor;
- acquisition of NVQs (National Vocational Qualifications) in relevant catering subjects;
- finding a site for possible acquisition by the company for a new outlet: if a site visit was made by the estates team a certain number of points were awarded; if the site was acquired, then a substantial further number of points were given;
- relevant suggestions made to improve some aspect of customer service or systems: almost any suggestion could receive a small number of points; points for an implemented suggestion varied according to its significance;
- knowing 100 customers by name and their favourite drink;
- spot awards by the pub manager or other more senior manager;
- long service awards based on service of over two years.

The catering industry has people in what are commonly regarded as low-value jobs potentially with associated low esteem. A central theme in this scheme was to find things for people to succeed at to build their own level of confidence and self-esteem. That was the philosophy of having a range of different things, each of which could provide points, including acquiring NVQs for people who otherwise had no qualifications of any kind.

Pilot

The programme was piloted with over 100 pubs against a similar-size control group. Compared with the control group, the pilot group sales growth increased by 3 per cent, profit by 9 per cent, and the customer care score – measured by customer survey – increased by 7 per cent. These numbers were very persuasive and six months later the scheme was launched across the rest of the pubs and restaurants.

Launch materials

Particular care was taken over the quality of the materials and communications. The scheme was launched with a series of road-shows to ensure that everyone understood it and each of the 10,000 employees got a copy of the catalogue. They each received a monthly statement showing their points balance. The programme was very well received. The perceived value by employees of the catalogue gifts was high, and the expected cost of gifts on average was over £250 ($375) per employee. The quality of the materials was seen as key to the success of the scheme. It reflected the sort of quality associated with customers, the message being that employees are important and we have gone to as much care with this scheme as if it had been something for our external customers.

Manager flexibility

The pub managers had a certain allocation of points vouchers that they could use as they wished to support their goals. The vouchers were allocated on the basis of the pub's turnover and appear within each unit's profit and loss account. Managers typically used them to recognize a particular example of good customer service, or as part of some other promotion. For example, one manager gave one point for every four packs of onion rings sold; the sales of onion rings in that pub went up by 1,000 per cent. Although this is an example of a direct incentive to increase sales, it is also fun and introduces some challenge and interest for the staff concerned.

Area managers and other senior manager had a points 'cheque book' from which they could write a 'cheque' for points to give to any employee to recognize something special that a manager had observed. For example, a senior manager wrote out a points cheque when he was in a pub and observed a member of staff dealing particularly well with a disabled customer. He wrote a second when someone in the central finance department provided him with some important data very fast within very tight deadlines.

Manager incentives

Pub managers were also eligible for prizes through the catalogue. The factors used were similar to those for their staff, with the addition of a food hygiene factor. They could receive a cheque for points from their area manager for some particular one-off achievement or success. In some cases an area manager gave a cheque to recognize the achievements of a whole team in a pub, including the manager. Area managers themselves received points based on the achievement of a range of factors, again similar to those for other staff, including sales, return on investment, customer service, new site recommendation, long service and suggestions to the suggestion scheme. In addition, there was an area manager of the quarter award that recognized an individual for overall achievement in the quarter.

The key mechanism

New staff in the pubs and restaurants were initially on a training rate of pay with a move to a higher rate with the acquisition of skills. There was no performance-related pay based on individual performance. The catalogue system was the key lever used to carry relevant messages. It was seen as having immediacy in linking reinforcement of behaviour through catalogue points that an annual pay award could not achieve.

Retention

There has been a positive effect on retention. People may have stayed simply because the scheme may have made the organization a better place to work; short-term retention may have been positively affected by people staying a little longer to acquire a particular gift. There was a high level of seasonal work in the industry, which meant that there was a benefit to the company if it could attract back good workers from last season. Any points in an individual's account when they left were frozen and reactivated on their return.

Other non-cash incentives

Reducing absence rates

Most organizations believe that attendance issues should be dealt with within the management framework. One reason for basic pay is for people to be at work. But there are examples of non-cash incentives being used in the public sector to help reduce absenteeism. The private sector has on average much lower absence rates, 6.4 days sick leave a year, than the public sector with an average of 9.7 days a year (Absence Management Survey, 2009). Some public sector organizations have sought to help address this with non-cash incentives.

Royal Mail had a problem with absence, particularly with postal workers in sorting offices. They introduced a non-cash incentive to encourage higher attendance. Workers with a very high attendance rate were entered into a draw for a Ford Focus car. They have given away 37 cars since introducing the scheme, but have seen absence rates fall from 6.1 per cent to 4.8 per cent. In addition, 74 employees have also won £2,000 ($3,000) holiday vouchers.

The fire service in Liverpool introduced a similar scheme to help reduce absence. Firefighters who attain 100 per cent attendance in a year are entered into a prize draw for a Honda Jazz car. There is also a draw for £1,000 ($1,500) for 100 per cent attendance over three months.

The Driver and Vehicle Licensing Agency runs a more modest scheme. Staff can enter the 'In to Win' prize draw for an extra day's holiday for high attendance in a month.

In each case a relatively small reduction in absence rates can have a huge positive impact on productivity and service. In the first two examples the organizations have been able to control costs but still offer an attractive and substantial value non-cash incentive by using a prize draw. The success of the National Lottery and further spin-off lotteries suggests why this approach has been able to have such a positive impact even though employees were in for a chance to win the non-cash incentive rather than definitely receive something for achieving low absence.

Incentivizing customers

Although not strictly within the remit of this book as it relates to incentivizing customers rather than employees, a non-cash incentive run by a housing association is also interesting. Irwell Valley Housing Association provides homes to over 20,000 people in Greater Manchester. But they had 70 per cent of their 5,000 tenants identified as poor payers. The housing association introduced 'Gold service membership' for those who paid their rent on time and abided by the terms of their tenancy agreement. They received a point worth £1 ($1.50) for every week that they achieved this. The points were credited to a special account and could be spent at a number of participating retailers. The result is that now the number of poor payers has reduced from 70 per cent to 30 per cent.

KEY JOBS TO DO

- Review the time spans over which individuals and teams have impact.
- Ensure any incentives are aligned with the time span.
- Consider different non-cash prizes for shorter periods.

Chapter nine
Conclusions and action plan

> *If you are going to sweep the stairs, start at the top.*
> **STEPHEN COLLEY**

THIS CHAPTER COVERS

- summary of key issues raised;
- action plan.

Conclusions

This book has tried to explain how to use non-cash awards to best effect as part of recognition and incentives. Each organization will have its own approach and as I said at the start, 'best fit' is more important than 'best practice'. But here I have listed the essence of the points I have tried to make in the book. If you consider each of these carefully you should be able to develop and run effective programmes.

Recognition

- Create a culture where you celebrate successes.
- Turn 'values' and 'behaviours' into stories.

- Consider carefully the impact and relationship between the new recognition programme(s) and existing HR programmes such as reward, performance management and learning and development.
- Start with the day-to-day/informal low-key line-manager-based programmes before bringing in any more formal programmes.
- Issue support and simple guidelines to managers, but do not use specific goals or measurable objectives as the criteria for recognition awards.
- Build recognition into your learning and development programmes for managers.
- Build on existing informal programmes that some line managers may already be running.
- Provide budget and infrastructure for a range of relatively low-value non-cash awards that can be matched to the person and the achievement.
- Try to make it as easy as possible for managers to source gifts and prizes, perhaps by using a third-party provider.
- Be very wary of simply buying an off-the-shelf recognition system.
- Encourage recognition to be delivered in an open and public way immediately after the event; it should be sincere and should match the award to the person and the achievement.
- Do not try to limit recognition to a budget or a quota.
- Avoid recognition programmes that are time bound, like employee of the month.
- Do not try to measure the success of a programme simply by the number of awards made, but do monitor the trend of usage.
- Use engagement surveys and exit interviews over time to monitor the impact of recognition strategies.
- If you are going to have some form of panel, consider using previous winners, rather than senior managers, to make decisions on those to receive awards.

Incentives

- Look at how you can use non-cash to support your cash incentive programmes.

- Use non-cash for short-term competitions and targets.
- Remember the value of social recognition of achievement as part of the incentive design.

Both

- Monitor the programmes and expect to refresh them regularly.
- Ensure you cover the tax issues for non-cash awards.

Action plan

- Review rationale for considering a recognition programme – survey evidence, exit interviews, management views, etc.
- Research – visit other organizations with recognition programmes; read about them: look at the References section at the back of this book.
- Discuss outline ideas with key stakeholders in the organization; agree concept in principle.
- Form design and implementation project team.
- Define aims of the programme – medium-term aims and overall success; establish what success indicators will be.
- Consider how you will explain the relationship between the recognition programme and other HR programmes, particularly reward.
- Establish outline budget.
- Consider using third-party provider.
- Develop scheme structure – who can recognize who, level of awards, etc.
- Review opportunity for sourcing awards – in house or outsource?
- Agree proposals with senior team as appropriate – timing, budget, etc.
- Develop programme guidelines and launch publicity.
- Launch.
- Review regularly; monitor both programme and success indicators.

KEY JOBS TO DO

● Consider carefully all of the points made and see how you can apply them.

Chapter ten
Case studies

In this final chapter I provide 10 case studies illustrating how different organizations use recognition and non-cash reward. The case study organizations are:

- 3;
- BIS;
- Comet;
- Edexcel;
- Great Ormond Street Hospital;
- Haringey Council;
- KPMG;
- Prudential;
- Sky;
- Standard Chartered Bank.

This is a mixture of public and private sector organizations of different sizes and in different sectors. Some operate globally and some only within the UK. There is a wide range of practice amongst the case study organizations; that is why I have chosen them. Throughout the book, I have referred to different elements of these case studies to provide examples of practice to illustrate some of the points I have made.

Most organizations regularly review their schemes and make small or large changes to them as they learn about how to make them more effective in meeting their aims. Therefore we need to understand that the case studies in this section are a snapshot in time and almost certainly will have changed to a greater or lesser extent after the cases were written.

The case studies show how different approaches are taken based on the history, culture and views of the case study organizations. You will be able to consider what aspects of each, if any, might work in your own organization. But remember that just because something seems to be working, or at least is being used, in one organization does not mean that it will have a similar impact in another.

I believe that we should look for 'best fit', rather than 'best practice'. Where 'best practice' may exist it is understanding the vital role that recognition plays in employee engagement. But after that, it is the context that allows one programme to work well in one place rather than another. The case studies represent a wide range of practice, so look at them critically with your understanding of where your organization is now and where it is trying to go.

3

Background

3 is a large mobile phone business that is part of Hutchison Whampoa Limited, a Hong Kong-based global conglomerate. Globally, Hutchison Whampoa has 3G operations in Australia, Austria, Denmark, Hong Kong, Ireland, Italy, Macau, Sweden as well as the UK, and markets its services under the global brand '3'.

3 has some 3,200 employees in the UK, of whom 2,000 are in the retail business, most in the 310 stores. The UK business was launched 3 March 2003.

3 operate three main recognition programmes: Thank you cards, Round of applause, and Oscars@3.

Thank you cards

Anyone can use this to thank anyone else in the business, based on three simple behaviours:

- taking responsibility;
- keeping your word;
- being open and honest.

They may also use the cards for a general Thank you where it does not link to a specific behaviour.

Originally people completed a physical card, but in 2008 the process went on the intranet and now thanks can be delivered via mobile phones. All employees have a company mobile phone and 3 were already delivering information on their flexible benefits plan, 'Just rewards' via mobile phones. So it is easy and appropriate to deliver recognition messages via this core company product. It is also a very efficient medium as so many employees are based in the shops. It is also considered effective, as electronic media via texts, picture messages or social media sites (Facebook, Twitter) delivered to their mobile phone is a natural and typically first choice for most of the employees at 3. The average age of 3 employees in the UK overall is 29 and in retail it is 26: a generation that has grown up with mobile phones. Feedback after the use of mobiles to deliver the thank you message was positive and 3 found the usage went up.

Thank you cards are on the '3 mobile intranet'. The individual searches for the name of the person they want to thank and selects the appropriate-design electronic card. They fill in a free text message of thanks and send it. Here are three examples of Thank you card messages:

> A huge thank you for all your help and support to my team in my absence with care calls and back to works, etc. Really appreciated!

> Just wanted to say thanks for taking ownership of a case that I was struggling to deal with and arranging to contact the customer so that their issues may be addressed by someone with sufficient knowledge in the technical field. Many thanks again.

> Hi, I would to take the time to thank you. You are always a great support and you always go out your way to offer this. You are a great 3 ambassador and advocate for quality and customer service as well as the 3 brand. Thank you.

Details of every Thank you card are also sent to the relevant director, who selects some winners each month. In 2009, 2,822 Thank yous were sent and there were 120 (4.3 per cent) winners. The winners receive a congratulatory e-mail from the director and 50 points that they can redeem through an online catalogue provided by an external third-party. A point is worth around £1 ($1.50). A wide range of activities, gifts and vouchers is available. 3 have found that vouchers are overwhelmingly the most popular option.

The costs are charged to the local director's budget and 3 settle the tax liability through their PSA.

Round of applause

This tier is for people who have really made a significant difference to the success of the company and displayed top-class behaviour. Typically it should be for a significant piece of work outside their day job. The person nominating has to get their director's sign-off (financial approval) to give someone a Round of applause. Although anyone can give a Round of applause to anyone, around 90 per cent are from managers who give them to members of their team. These awards are therefore similar to a spot bonus.

The individual may receive an e-mail with the Round of applause, but face-to-face communication is encouraged. Round of applause can be used for both teams and individuals and 3 find that there is a roughly even split between team and individual awards. Teams are typically five to 10 members. This is a high level of use of awards for teams, as most organizations use many more individual than team awards. 3 frequently use project teams and stores naturally are small teams of five to 10. The culture of 3 may also make it more common practice to recognize team success. Here are three examples of Round of applause messages:

> Thank you so much for all your hard work in getting us to the point where we have a company plan for the next two years. This has been a great team effort and one that you have all worked really hard on achieving, so thank you!

> You ensured the retail staff were able to demo Skype in store at very short notice. Taking outstanding responsibility and turning around quickly (keeping your word). Thanks.

> Thanks for spotting an issue with our proofs policy, and working closely with the fraud team to suggest improvements. You saw a problem and took responsibility for helping to solve it.

Unlike the Thank you cards, where only some will receive a non-cash award in the form of points, with the Round of applause the individual will be given between 100 and 300 points, again with the tax settled by the company.

Thank you cards and Round of applause awards are promoted together. The introduction to them on the intranet says:

> If you know of someone who has done a great job, then why not add an extra shine to their day and give them a 3Cheers Thank you card or Round of applause to show your appreciation! We all make a difference to each other's working life and 3Cheers is one of the ways we let people know that we value their contribution. So if you see someone taking responsibility, keeping their word, being open and honest or just doing a good job, this is how you can thank them.

In 2009, 225 Round of applause awards were made.

Oscars@3

Oscars@3 recognizes the 'best of the best' from all of the Thank you card and Round of applause recipients in the financial year (the calendar year). In February, lists of all winners within each division, with justifications, are sent to the relevant divisional director, who is asked to select the top two or three for their division. They are asked to choose winners whose overall behaviour and contribution to the business have been outstanding and will be recognized by their peers as worthy winners. In 2009 there were 18 Oscar winners: two Thank you winners and one Round of applause winner for each of the six divisions.

The names of the winners go back to HR, who arrange a significant internal announcement using the 3 intranet. Winners receive a congratulatory e-mail from the CEO. They receive an engraved Tiffany crystal star, which many winners display on their desk, and a top-of-the-range mobile phone. The CEO with other directors takes the winners out to lunch. 3 pay for the travel and any accommodation costs of the winners attending the lunch. One side benefit is that the CEO and the other directors get direct access to people who may be working in relatively junior roles and can hear what these people, often with direct customer contact, think about things at 3.

Recognition links

3 have an annual staff survey run by MORI. Although there is no direct question on recognition, the results are very positive for reward and recognition combined in absolute terms and in comparison with comparator groups. Although there may not be a clear causal link between the recognition approach and these results, it may be reasonable to assume that the programmes have led to effective recognition reflected at least in part in the survey scores.

There is no formal link between the recognition awards and 3's more formal performance management system using an annual review. However, they can be brought up in discussion or in the pre self-assessment by the recipient as objective evidence particularly in relation to behavioural measures.

3 incorporate training about recognizing colleagues and team members across the range of workshops and programmes that they offer. Some of the programmes where this is covered are:

- *Focus (performance management)*. These workshops aim to support managers in agreeing objectives and development plans with their team members. These objectives should help the individual to understand their role and contribution to departmental – and business – success. It is also where their personal development plan will be agreed. This can include both business (development needed to do the job) and personal (longer-term career and/or professional) development. It is also a forum for giving and receiving feedback – which would include recognition of objectives completed, challenges met and obstacles overcome. There is also discussion about how to recognize and reward individual performance and behaviour. This includes formal and informal approaches, from the Thank you e-mails to saying thank you.
- *Fearless (introduction to management)*. This covers delegation, giving feedback and having courageous conversations. In the delegation section they consider the rationale for delegating specific tasks to individuals – the reasons can include offering interesting and challenging tasks as recognition. A follow-up

day includes a session on motivation, which links with recognition.

- *Team performance health check (TPHC)*. Quite a few teams have used the TPHC to understand how well their team is doing. There are statements in here about 'recognizing and celebrating success together'. The purpose is partially to raise awareness of these, and partially to embed them as being a key part of a team's success.

BIS

Background

The Department for Business, Innovation and Skills was created in June 2009 from the merger of the Department for Business, Enterprise and Regulatory Reform (BERR) and the Department for Innovation, Universities and Skills (DIUS). The mission of BIS is building a dynamic and competitive UK economy by: creating the conditions for business success; promoting innovation, enterprise and science; and giving everyone the skills and opportunities to succeed. The budget is around £22 billion ($33 billion) for 2009/ 2010, which makes BIS the sixth largest spending department in Whitehall. Top budget areas include funding for higher education, science and research, adult skills, support for business, and the Regional Development Agencies.

The department has around 3,500 staff in over 10 locations around the UK. It is structured into 12 management groups: Business, Economic and Policy Analysis, Fair Markets, Finance, Innovation and Enterprise (including the Better Regulation Executive), Legal Services, Operations and Change, Science and Research, Shareholder Executive, Strategy and Communications, UK Trade and Investment, and Universities and Skills.

BIS run a regular people survey, which is the same across the civil service, and in the 2009 survey the results suggested a high level of manager recognition. There was a 78 per cent positive response to the statement, 'My manager recognizes when I have done my job well.' This is slightly better than the civil service overall positive response to this question of 76 per cent.

Initial programme

In 2007 the then chief operations officer (COO), Hilary Douglas, introduced a simple recognition scheme for the corporate centre of what was BERR at the time, comprising 320 people. The scheme was known as 'Hilary's awards', but became the 'Corporate centre awards'. The scheme was introduced as part of a change to help to get people to work together more closely and to celebrate success. It was based on the BERR values:

- making a difference;
- working together;
- 'It starts with me.'

Anyone in the centre could nominate by e-mail any individual or team for recognition for something they had done within one of these values. The individual might or might not know that they had been nominated. A small panel including the COO reviewed the nominations for the last six months and identified a winner, or possibly two, for each of the three categories. Although there were no formal criteria for the selection, the panel wanted to see that the individual had clearly supported the value. They gave weight to where there was a positive impact on an internal customer and to cross-team working.

A short presentation ceremony was organized every six months which would be publicized internally and would be open for anyone to attend. Around 100 people would typically attend. The winner for each category would be invited to step forward on stage and what they had done to be nominated would be read out. They would be presented with a certificate and a small cash sum of up to £50 ($75), which was taxed through payroll. Photographs were taken and used for internal publicity. Those attending seem very pleased for their colleagues who had won. The winners were often people doing low-profile jobs who would otherwise not get much recognition.

BIS also operate three other recognition plans based on those from the old legacy departments (BERR and DIUS), which are outlined below. But BIS are in the process of reviewing all of the recognition awards across the department as part of a strategic review of reward and recognition with the aim of giving a more coherent approach.

The permanent secretary's award

This has been created to reward and celebrate teams who deliver the highest-quality policy work. The awards recognize confident policy-making principles such as innovation, robustness and customer focus in policy development. All nominations should also reflect the BIS values.

Anyone at any level within the department, including members of the team themselves, can nominate a team using a standard form. A 'team' includes anyone at any grade and in any role who made a significant contribution to the policy project (eg press officers, analysts, support staff).

The permanent secretary announces and confers awards on the winners at a ceremony in the ministerial conference suite. The winners' projects are promoted as case studies on the policy portal and through internal media such as BIS TV screens. The ceremony is open to the nominees, their senior leadership and all BIS staff on a 'first come first served' basis to network and share good practice and celebrate the success of colleagues.

The reward consists of an award to be spent on a specific event for the team (eg Christmas lunch, visit to London Zoo, tea at the Dorchester). The awards are made once or twice a year. The number of teams winning will depend to a large extent on numbers being put forward.

Special awards

These are flexible one-off 'spot bonuses', with their origin in BERR. They are aimed at recognizing exceptional performance over a few weeks or months that is not typically reflected in the annual performance review and associated pay review. This could be, for example, involvement in a special project or managing a crisis. Anyone could nominate anyone else for a special award. There is no limit on the size or number of special bonuses other than a budget limit of historically 0.4 per cent of the annual pay bill. A bonus must be authorized at an appropriate level depending on its value. The person authorizing sends a letter to the person receiving the award explaining the reason. Awards are paid through payroll and are subject to PAYE.

In-year bonus

In-year bonuses can be awarded any time for contributions to delivering objectives that also demonstrate the BIS values. This bonus system originated in DIUS. Anyone can nominate anyone else for an award via a panel set up within their directorate. To provide transparency, each directorate is encouraged to establish a panel of at least four people at different levels to review and agree the awards. Awards are typically £250, £500 or £750 ($375, $750, $1,125). There is no limit to the size or number of awards, but they are limited to a budget of approximately 0.7 per cent of the pay bill. They need to be appropriately approved and are paid through payroll. An individual receiving an award receives a letter explaining why.

To complement the in-year bonus there is also an instant reward available to recognize people demonstrating the BIS values. These are in the form of retail vouchers, normally £25 or £50 ($38 or $75). Anyone can nominate anyone for an instant award. To try to keep the process reasonably fast, each directorate appoints an individual to approve them (rather than a panel). The individual then receives a note informing them that they have received an award. BIS covers the tax and NIC directly with HMRC.

Performance management

The recognition programmes are separate from the formal performance management system. BIS see the recognition as an immediate award for good work, whereas performance management is around helping drive continuous improvement. But they would expect that any recognition is likely to be brought up in the performance review.

Comet Group plc

Background

Comet is a leading electrical retailer and is part of Europe's second largest electrical group – KESA. They have over 250 stores plus an internet shopping business and all of the support and infrastructure needed, such as delivery centres, after-sales service centres and so on. Comet employ some 10,000 people (colleagues) in the UK.

Comet have simple, well communicated vision, value and behaviours integrated within the overall framework of 'Our journey.' These are:

- *Our vision*: Britain's most trusted electrical specialist;
- *Our value*: trustworthy;
- *Our behaviours*: deep knowledge, care for every detail, passion for service, individual attitude.

The vision, value and behaviours permeate everything Comet does and are built into the various programmes that aim to promote the right culture for the organization. For example, they are used in colleague communications, within the performance management and appraisal system, and colleagues are encouraged to challenge behaviours and initiatives against them.

Recognition is seen as an integral part of reward and engagement at Comet. They work hard to distinguish between:

- reward versus recognition; and
- the everyday versus the extra mile.

Comet have a large number of different recognition programmes, from a simple 'thank you' through to more formal high-profile events. The main programmes are summarized below.

Thank you cards

Comet had various unofficial, ad hoc recognition activities happening and in 2007 they pulled together best practice from around the business. The launch of the Comet printed Thank you cards was an integral part of this, which came from an idea from various managers and colleagues who had already been providing and sending their own versions. They were considered to be just one of a number of key building blocks important to helping foster a general culture of recognition, however big or small the activity being recognized.

Thank you cards are simple cards printed in a pad format, which have a single fold so that they can stand up on a desk. They are made available for managers, colleagues and customers to recognize something someone has done at any time. These might be quite small things; it is up to the person giving the recognition to write whatever they wish in the way of thanks and recognition. There is no formal link to other recognition schemes or any gift or award. However, line managers may choose to use them as part of any local recognition scheme such as a store 'colleague of the month'. The main point is just to encourage sincere, simple thanks for something that was done and was appreciated. It is up to the recipient to display their Thank you cards as they wish. It is clear that many people value receiving this sort of thanks as they are often displayed around the offices and on noticeboards. One individual had all her Thank you cards on display all the way around her desk cubicle. Here are three quotes from Thank you cards from different business areas:

> Head office. Richard, thank you so much for stepping in to cover the phones in my department to allow the team to have important time out for their business update and team building today. You showed your excellent 'passion for service' by not only helping us to maintain the level of our call-answering service to our internal customers, but also by seeking a full resolution to any queries on the spot rather than simply taking messages and passing them on. Not always easy when working in a department that is not your natural home. This meant our customers were not only 'heard' but also went away 'answered' in a timely manner. Your efforts were very much appreciated both by myself and my team.

Retail stores. Mohammed, thanks for postponing your day off last week at such short notice to cover Mandy's absence and finish merchandising the new promotions, making sure that we were ready for our customers. I know that you had plans with your family that you then rearranged so I really appreciate the sacrifice you made – great 'individual attitude!

Services. Dear Joanna, just a quick note to pass on my thanks for the 'care for every detail' that you showed when dealing with Mr Kemp's TV. He has told me that you were really thorough and also picked up that he was experiencing another unrelated problem. He said that you politely helped him identify this as a 'user error' rather than a technical fault and then talked him through the solution. This saved us later booking unnecessary additional time to fix a perceived issue and so avoided a frustrated customer. He specifically made a point of phoning me to say how delighted he was with the great all-round service he received. Well done!

Comet stars

This is a centrally driven recognition programme that started in 2006 and runs for the three month 'peak' business period of November to January. It is well publicized across the business, using posters, screen savers, intranet and *Comet Life*, the company magazine.

Any colleague may nominate anyone else who they believe has displayed something 'really special', going the 'extra mile' and demonstrating one of the four behaviours:

- deep knowledge;
- care for every detail;
- passion for service;
- individual attitude.

The nomination must be for something real that supports the business. It is interesting to note that Comet are looking to reinforce and motivate colleagues to deliver the four key behaviours especially at their peak trading period. This may be in contrast with sales-driven commission schemes in operation at other retailers. Although Comet do use a range of sales-related bonuses, they do not pay direct commission to their sales colleagues for products sold.

They use a Comet star card with a personal message to the colleague being recognized, completing the section starting, 'I recognize you as a Comet star because... ', which they give to the individual. They also complete an attached card with the name of the colleague being recognized and their own details and complete a short section: 'Tell us the story of what they did... '. This needs to be signed by their line manager, '...so that they are aware of the fantastic job that your colleague has done.' The nomination card is sent to the reward and benefits team who manage the process. Comet typically receive around 5,000 nominations. All stars are reviewed centrally and the 'Top 100' receive a Comet lapel badge, which is presented by their manager. From the Top 100, nine colleagues from across the business are selected by the operating board to receive a regional/business area trophy which is presented by a director. They also receive an additional week's holiday. One of these nine colleagues becomes the 'Ultimate star' and also receives an extra week's pay. The winners are featured on the company intranet and in *Comet Life*.

Manager recognition toolkit

Comet issue a recognition toolkit to all managers. This is written simply and provides practical ideas on how best to recognize colleagues. It also provides other information and data to allow managers to recognize birthdays, start dates and 100 per cent attendance, as they wish. It contains:

- *A–Z guide to recognition at Comet*. Some simple hints and tips and guidance on recognition to help managers make it a success in their area. They are put together with the help of some of the Comet managers across the business who have developed their own best way of recognizing people. There is guidance on a number of areas, including 'what some great managers do' and 'the four key elements of recognition that really work'.
- *Book*. An easy-to-read published book on recognition that provides easy-to-use, inexpensive recognition ideas, hints and tips and pieces of advice to re-energize colleagues.

- Birthday and start date listings for their teams as well as some birthday cards for them to send.
- 100 per cent attendance listing.
- *Colleague of the month template.* A simple template that the manager can use to run a colleague of the month scheme if they wish. They provide a poster that the manager can display as appropriate. It has space to insert a picture and description of the successful colleague/s. Other guidance is provided for the manager.
- *Positive impact questionnaire.* A simple questionnaire with 15 questions to help the manager consider what can help to identify areas to enhance positive impact. This is based on the idea that every day you have an opportunity to recognize someone or have a positive impact on the colleagues in your team.
- Guide to the tax implications of local gifts.

Millionaires club

This recognizes the sales colleagues (not store managers) who take more than £1 million ($1.5 million) in sales during each financial year. This is calculated pro rata for part timers. Individuals can see how they are doing each week in relation to the £1 million ($1.5 million) (and other measures and KPIs used for other incentive arrangements) online by logging on to the intranet in their store. All those who achieve the £1 million ($1.5 million) of sales join the Millionaires club and are invited to an event to celebrate. This is typically a day out followed by a gala dinner and an overnight stay. Members of the club also receive a badge with an 'M' symbol. Senior managers and directors attend the event.

Comet capture ideas and tips from these top salespeople. Typically they are asked to submit their tips over the few weeks following the celebration event. These learnings are used in different ways to help improve business performance. Some of the ideas may be fed back to relevant head office departments such as learning and development, who manage the 'Comet way of selling' training, and reward department, who devise sales reward programmes. Sales tips will also be promoted to other sales colleagues, for example using DVDs and the store intranet.

This is an example tip from a Millionaire sales colleague:

> When approaching customers in the store, I tend to favour something like 'Hello, is someone looking after you?' rather than the more direct 'Can I help you?' as it feels more natural. Customers are all different, so the way I talk to and approach them differs too, rather than using one approach for everyone. Giving customers enough space and time to settle down is also important, as is customer awareness: looking for customer 'need help' signals, eg touching product or focusing in on a product.

Store manager of the year

This programme was introduced for store managers as they did not have a formal recognition programme. They need to demonstrate success in the various criteria for measurement, which are around sales, profit, customer service, mystery shopper results and other KPIs related to Comet's vision, value and behaviours. It is a competitive population with regularly published league tables showing how people are doing. The top store manager in each area is invited to a long weekend away with their partner or a friend. The first day of the weekend event usually consists of an award ceremony, photographs and a gala dinner, etc. There is one overall winner, but there is no additional award or prize, simply the recognition. Day two is generally for the managers and their partners/friends to relax and enjoy themselves, with check out on day three.

Bright sparks

'Bright sparks' is a scheme used to generate and recognize ideas that could improve sales, save the company money or help Comet give the best possible customer service. It is open to all colleagues who can send their ideas through to a dedicated e-mail address by the end of April each year. Up to 10 are shortlisted in each business area, eg retail, services and head office.

After shortlisting, finalists are invited to present their idea to a panel of senior managers, directors and other key business personnel in May. There are winners by business area and then an overall winner, who are announced in June. Comet budget up to a total of £2,000 ($3,000), which is allocated depending on the impact of the ideas on the business. It is paid in June through payroll but may be tax free within HMRC limits. The leading ideas are publicized throughout Comet via the intranet, *Comet Life* magazine and communication cascades.

Comet typically get over 1,000 ideas each year. One previous winner was a store colleague who wrote a piece of PC software that stores could use to download product information direct from the Comet site to create correctly formatted replacement point-of-sale product ticketing. This meant that when changes were required they could be updated much more quickly than the lengthier process involving additional work from head office to each store. It was a solution that was quicker, easier, accurate, efficient and money saving.

Recognition in context

Based on all the work Comet have done over the years on recognition, they have identified their five top do's and don'ts:

Do:
- Relate to the culture of the business.
- Link to company values.
- Give responsibility to individuals and line managers.
- Learn from how people have used the tools.
- Make it simple to use and understand.

Don't:
- Assume everyone likes to be recognized in the same way.
- Assume everyone likes to be recognized at all.
- Assume it will solve all business challenges.
- Make it bureaucratic.
- Underestimate the power of a simple thank you.

Comet have been using an annual employee survey, 'Your opinion counts', since 1999. Although the questions they use in the survey have changed slightly over the years, there has always been one relating to recognition. The main question used is, 'My manager recognizes and acknowledges when I have done my job well.' Comet have monitored the recognition score in both absolute and relative (compared with other companies) terms.

Comet's recognition and engagement score has improved steadily over the years. By 2009 they scored around the 75th percentile, ie compared with other companies 75 per cent had a score lower than Comet.

As recognition is a core part of the way things are done at Comet, they have been developing ways to identify those people who do it well to be held up as role models for others in the business to aspire to. Therefore Comet recognize people who recognize others.

Comet cover their recognition programmes briefly at induction for all new colleagues. They also cover motivation and recognition in their managers' workshop sessions for new managers once or twice a year.

While there are quite deliberately no hard and fast rules laid down around how, when or how often an individual should recognize other Comet colleagues, there is nevertheless a degree of measurement of this through the performance appraisal process. For example, one of the points for consideration on a Comet middle manager's appraisal document is whether the manager 'demonstrates an understanding of individual needs and motivators in the way they engage and recognize colleagues'. The individual is asked to evidence what they have done in this area. Similarly, while colleagues do not 'score' or 'lose' points based on the number of Thank you cards or Comet stars they receive, they would be encouraged to offer any received as evidence during their appraisal when discussing their 'passion for service' (summarized from Comet vision, values and behaviours).

Edexcel

Background

Edexcel is the UK's largest qualifications-awarding body offering academic and vocational qualifications and testing to schools, colleges, employers and other places of learning in the UK and internationally. Its business is to provide materials, consulting and advice to education providers and associated stakeholders. They offer a wide range of learning programmes, from academic qualifications – such as the 'gold standard' GCEs (A levels) and GCSEs – to vocational and business learning and adult literacy and numeracy qualifications. Edexcel had been a not-for-profit organization until May 2003 when it was acquired by Pearson plc.

In 2008, Edexcel delivered 8.2 million exam scripts in over 85 countries. Their general qualifications taken internationally include GCSEs, AS and A Levels, IGCSEs and O Levels. Vocational qualifications include NVQ and BTEC from entry level to Higher National Diplomas. Edexcel employs some 1,200 people in two main locations but with other staff spread across the UK.

In March 2004 Edexcel introduced a three-tier recognition programme to help managers recognize excellent performance, promote its values and create 'a bit of a buzz'. Each of the three tiers, Star awards, Star value awards and Star exceptional awards, is described below.

Star cards

Star cards are to encourage anyone to recognize the great things done by anyone else in the business. A simple e-mail-based 'thank you card' can be used to send a message directly to someone you wish to recognize and thank. The guidance on Star cards says, 'Anyone can say a simple and heartfelt thank you to their colleagues. If you feel that someone has made a difference and this should be acknowledged, then here is your chance to do so.' Average number of nominations for the Star cards is between 250 and 350 per month. Here is an example of the sort of message given on a Star card:

> Arthur, I just wanted to thank you for your outstanding efforts over the last few days. In addition to your normal work you have managed to prepare a report on new assessment initiatives in Australia and New Zealand, which will suggest new ideas for us to adapt for use in Edexcel. Your work is much appreciated.

A copy of the e-mail is automatically sent to the administrator in HR via Microsoft Outlook. Each month the names of those receiving a thank you card are entered into a prize draw. When launched there were three prizes of £100 ($150) awarded each month. This was then changed to vary the number of prizes with the number of thank you cards sent in the month, so that three prizes were drawn when there were fewer than 150 cards, four prizes for 150–200 and five prizes when more than 200 cards were sent in the month. The £100 ($150) was paid gross through payroll and subject to tax and NI. This has now changed to £30 ($45) John Lewis vouchers, of which 10 prizes are drawn each month. The vouchers are bought directly from John Lewis. The cost of this is budgeted centrally and tax is covered by the company through its PSA. This part of the recognition programme is run by the communications team, who also manage the internal communications for the division. They ensure that the names of the winners are featured in the regular electronic employee newsletter.

Edexcel issue a weekly newsletter, *RoundUp*, which is sent to all employees every Friday by e-mail. Each week it contains a section called 'Question of the week', which is usually about something in the news, a business issue or work-related topic. In June 2009 they used the Question of the week section to ask people about the Star scheme, to gauge the level of understanding and usage of the Star card system. Recipients could simply click on the link to post their response. Responses were collated automatically and the results were reported back to staff the following Friday (19 June 2009). They found that 70 per cent of people understood when and how to send a Star card; 43 per cent sent one to five cards a month and 3 per cent sent six to 10 cards a month, while 54 per cent had sent none; 68 per cent of respondents had received at least one Star card; and 10 per cent of respondents had won a Star card prize.

Star value awards

While the Star cards may be used by anyone, Star value awards are for managers to use for individuals or teams and are linked directly to the company values. Originally the link was to the Edexcel values, but in early 2007 they were switched to the Pearson values. Staff can be particularly recognized by their manager for actions and behaviours that exceed expectations and embody the Pearson company values:

- brave;
- decent;
- imaginative;
- supportive.

This is an example of a message used for a Star value award:

> I would like to nominate Jim for a Star value award. Recently, Jim has been working on a job where he has been under pressure from a number of internal customers to produce a quick result. Jim took the view that while speed of response was important, it was more important to get it right from the customer's perspective as well as meeting the internal timescale. He did not take the easy option and bow to the pressure and cut corners but stuck to the quality route and maintained the required standards as well as meeting the required timescale. I believe that this demonstrates a high degree of integrity and effort on Jim's part.

The value of awards is between £25 and £150 ($38 and $225). They can take the form of specific 'gifts' such as a meal out, flowers, theatre tickets, or vouchers or cash. The manager completes a simple form with information about why the award is being proposed and the proposed value, which their boss has to approve. It is for the manager to decide the form of the award and to arrange the purchase of any non-cash awards. The cost is borne by the manager's cost centre and for non-cash awards, tax and NI are covered by the company through their PSA. Cash awards are paid through payroll and are subject to tax and NIC. It is then up to the manager how the awards will be made. Face-to-face communication is encouraged. Managers often find appropriate events such as team meetings at which to present the awards.

Star exceptional awards

Star exceptional awards are for employees or teams who have shown outstanding drive and dedication in support of company values and business goals. They are normally awarded to someone who has worked in such a manner over a substantial time frame or concentrated period for work that has significantly improved the business. Nominations may be made by senior managers and directors using a simple nomination form which must be approved by the divisional director. The HR director also reviews all of these awards.

This is one of the nominations for a Star exceptional award for the new product development team:

> I would like to nominate the NPD team for a Star exceptional award. They have managed to develop a complete new product for the emerging South American market in record time. To do so, they had to work across the whole business – bringing together expertise from qualifications development, assessment, e-business and finance to deliver a ready-for-market product, which will exactly fit the identified market need and deliver significant financial return very quickly because of the ease of assessment. I recommend that they receive an appropriate reward to recognize their efforts, which have truly been above and beyond all our expectations.

The awards are in the form of taxable cash bonuses paid through payroll, but positioned within the recognition framework. Although there is no formal cap, the value is typically up to £3,000 ($4,500), which is covered by the department.

Recognition links

There is no formal link between the recognition awards and the Edexcel performance management system. However, Edexcel expects line managers to take account of any recognition awards when assessing performance. Because of the way the system works, if someone other than the line manager nominates someone for a Star card, their line manager might not know about it, but it is reasonable to expect the individual recipient to bring the award to the attention of their manager as an input for their review.

The recognition scheme is mentioned briefly in the induction for all new employees. Edexcel have a series of e-learning modules for new managers, which amongst other things include a section on how to motivate, recognize and reward your people. This covers the role of the recognition schemes in the motivation and recognition of people in their teams.

Great Ormond Street Hospital

Background

The world-famous Great Ormond Street Hospital for Children NHS Trust (GOSH) is a national centre of excellence in the provision of specialist children's healthcare. They deliver the widest range of specialities of any children's hospital in the UK. They are the largest centre for research into childhood illness outside the USA and the largest centre for children's heart transplants in the world. With the University College London Hospitals, GOSH are the largest centre for children with cancer/leukaemia in Europe.

The GOSH Mission is to provide world-class clinical care and training, pioneering new research and treatments, in partnership with others for the benefit of children in the UK and worldwide. Their key value is 'The child, first and always'.

The hospital opened in 1852 as the Hospital for Sick Children. With only 10 beds, it was the first hospital in the UK dedicated to children. GOSH now have 29 wards and a total of 335 beds and treat over 22,000 inpatients and 77,000 outpatients a year. They do 10,600 scheduled operations and 2,635 unscheduled operations a year. GOSH have a total staff of some 3,000. This includes 315 doctors, 900 registered nurses and healthcare assistants, and 135 professionals allied to medicine (eg physiotherapists).

When the current chief executive was appointed in 2001, she was keen to introduce some form of recognition of the great things people do in GOSH as part of her view of the criticality to engage staff. This was within a new personal responsibility framework that set out the Trust's corporate values of openness, accountability and mutual respect.

Recognition programmes history

In 2003 a quarterly recognition scheme (staff recognition awards) was developed where anyone could nominate any individual or team for a recognition award for their contribution. The criteria for nominating or receiving an award were very broad, described in publicity as 'going the extra mile', and tied loosely to the values within the personal responsibility framework. Nominations for the quarter were reviewed and awards made for each quarter. These were vouchers to the value of £100 ($150) for the individual, and for the team funding for an event costing up to £500 ($750). However, it was felt that the quarterly awards required a lot of administration but achieved relatively few nominations. The scheme was not delivering the value and impact hoped for when launched.

For several years, GOSH had held an annual ceremony to celebrate the success of any member of staff in achieving an internal or external academic qualification, be it an NVQ or a PhD. Long service was also celebrated in this ceremony.

Current approach

Following a review in 2007, a combined approach to recognizing qualifications, long service and staff who had made a particular contribution was launched in 2008. There would be a single annual ceremony in May each year covering the three.

Nominations are encouraged from staff, patients, parents and carers for the staff awards in six categories as defined by GOSH:

- 'Zero to hero' is for an exceptional contribution to achieving their zero-harm targets.
- 'Bureaucracy buster' is a shining example of cutting red tape.
- 'Colleague of the year' is a special individual who improves the working lives of the people around them (nominations by staff only).
- 'Team of the year' work together to make a real difference to patients, families and/or staff.
- 'Manager of the year' is an exceptional manager who listens, motivates, empowers and helps the team to achieve their goals (nominations by staff only).
- 'Child and family award' is for a special individual or team nominated by a patient, parent or carer.

The Zero to hero award is particularly intended to support and celebrate the Trust's work on reducing errors and infections in patient care, which is a key part of the organization's major transformation programme.

There is a simple form available online or at nomination boxes on which the category and details of the nomination can be written. They can be dropped into nomination boxes at the hospital reception area, HR or other locations that see large footfall, such as outpatients departments. Alternatively, they can be sent to the chief executive or e-mailed to a dedicated e-mail address. Nominations need to be in by the end of April each year. The awards are publicized in the widely read staff newsletter, through all-staff weekly e-bulletins, and through e-mails targeted to line managers and cascaded within teams. The Trust's union representatives have also promoted the awards with their members.

The hospital has taken a deliberate decision to welcome nominations from staff as well as from patients and their families, since all staff, including those in corporate functions, are encouraged to consider themselves as being part of the team. However, the Trust is particularly keen to promote the awards to families. It does this via its website, and in 2010 for the first time used its Facebook page to direct people who want to make a nomination to this site.

HR undertake an initial review, sort out the nominations and compile them into a manageable format on Excel, including the verbatim nominations. They will, for example, ensure that the nominated individual is still employed by GOSH. All nominations are passed to a panel for consideration.

The panel has four members – the chief executive, director of nursing, chair of the staff side (unions) and head of patient involvement. The head of workforce planning and development, who oversees the scheme, acts as secretary to the panel and provides any advice and guidance as required. They agree a main award winner and usually two other shortlisted nominees for each category.

Each person who is nominated receives a letter of congratulations signed by the chief executive and inviting them to attend the annual award ceremony at the end of May. Those shortlisted and who have been chosen to receive an award are not told, but they are encouraged to attend and their manager will be asked to ensure they are released from work in order to do so.

Ceremony

Some 200 people typically attend the award ceremony, which is held in a large lecture hall at the end of the day, usually starting at 5 o'clock and lasting for about 40 minutes. The event is managed to keep it as short as possible without losing the positive impact of the recognition. So for example, for the long service element, people are asked to stand up in groups for their number of years' service and are applauded as a group.

The hospital's reputation has resulted in long-standing associations with celebrities, and it tries to invite someone who will be known to staff to the ceremony in order to present each award and have their photograph taken with winners.

The chief executive hosts the award ceremony. The staff awards are interspersed between the recognition of long service and achievement of qualifications. To help reflect that to some extent all of those nominated for a staff award are 'winners', the words 'winner' and 'runners-up' are not used in the presentation. Rather, there are typically two people named as 'shortlisted' and then, 'the person receiving the award is...'. The details of the nomination for each are read out by the chief executive, who then passes over to the celebrity to announce the recipient. Here are a few examples of some of the nominations made:

Nominations from staff:

- Nothing fazes A, she always has a kind word, however stressed everyone else is. No matter how busy she is, if one of the patients stops to say hello, she will always have a big hug and smile for them. The children love her. Her hard work and dedication deserve to be acknowledged. Works relentlessly above and beyond the call of duty.

- B is a wonderful example of a team player who not only ensures that the team maintains its high standard of work, but is also always there with tea, biscuits and a hug when difficult times occur. B is a unique and special individual who not only improves others' working lives but helps to inspire and encourage others, to get the best out of them.

- Not only does C excel in his duties, but he also treats everybody well and makes us all comfortable and proud to know him. He is also a 'cool cat'. He is an all-round 'good guy' and firm but fair. He is an outstanding manager. He is very supportive and ensures the teams are updated to make sure goals are met. He leads by example and goes beyond the scope of his duties. He is an excellent role model.

- D manages a large department with professionalism, authority yet empathy, integrity, fairness, encouragement, approachability and humour. She leads by example, her extensive knowledge base and professional achievements providing us all with a role model par excellence.

Nominations from patients and families:

- We were immediately struck by how efficient, organized, proactive and pre-emptive the team are. They are all of this and more. Clinical care at a personal level – they made so much time and effort to be approachable, friendly and caring. We feel they are a team at the top of their game. Very methodical, explain clearly to us what they are trying to achieve and we understand everything. This gives us so much reassurance and confidence. When we bump into anyone from the team they take time to chat; really helps to put us at ease.

- We would be pleased if E's hard work was recognized by the whole hospital for his care of patients, his prompt and consistent help for us (parents) and for his colleagues that work with him as everyone's job is easier when he is around. We do not know how to thank him.

The award is in the form of a certificate plus vouchers to the value of £100 ($150) for an individual. For a team, they may choose how to spend an amount of up to £500 ($750) on a team event. Most common is a team dinner. In each case any tax is settled by GOSH through their PSA.

For the Child and family award, the Trust contacts the family who made the winning nomination and invites them to attend the ceremony, if at all possible, and to participate in presenting the award. The Trust would pay reasonable travel or subsistence expenses to assist with this.

Nominations and publicity

After the ceremony, all attending are invited to stay for a short reception. Following the ceremony, the staff newsletter carries an article each month on one of the award recipients, outlining why they were nominated and how they felt at receiving the award.

Total numbers of nominations have increased but have not exceeded 200 a year since this scheme started. Although the Trust might wish to have more nominations, the quality of them is seen as very high. They believe that the feel-good effect is tremendous for the individual/team who is nominated, and indeed for the person who makes the nomination and sees someone they appreciated being recognized more widely.

GOSH work on increasing the publicity and getting the message out about the recognition programme, but would prefer to have a smaller number of nominations that allow them to see and collectively celebrate their outstanding staff rather than a larger number of fairly mediocre citations that are just saying that some-one does their job competently. Although GOSH recognize that it does not have to be either/or, they believe that their challenge is often to get people to recognize in themselves and each other that what they do is extraordinary when they work in an environment where the extraordinary is what they strive to achieve every day.

Recognition links

There is no formal link to the annual staff performance management system. But managers and staff members may bring their nomination for an award into any performance discussion.

Recognition is not covered directly within training and development, but appraisal training very much focuses on recognizing achievement as well as areas for development. The Trust has recently developed a coaching strand as part of its management development, which is about recognizing strengths and abilities. They also encourage staff to do 360-degree feedback.

Haringey Council

Background

Haringey employ over 8,000 people within five directorates and deliver over 700 different services to 226,000 residents in over 100,000 households in North London.

Haringey believes that its values are critical to its success and should be easily recognized in everything they do. The values should underpin their purpose and influence behaviours, systems and processes. The values are:

- Service – we work for the good of all our diverse communities.
- Integrity – we keep our promises.
- Improvement – we strive for excellence.
- Passion – we are passionate about our work and proud of what we do.
- One council – we deliver by working together.

Customer service

The majority of employees have a direct effect on the lives of the residents of Haringey. The council recognized that customer service was a critical component in helping to deliver on their values. There was a well-developed and established customer complaints system, but little captured the positive things being done within the council, other than a very low-profile customer compliments scheme. But given the significance of the customer experience, Haringey were interested in developing something that would make it easy for customers to praise staff who did their jobs exceptionally well. They believed that this would provide both a direct thank you to the staff concerned and direct customer feedback for the organization to learn from, alongside that provided by the complaints system.

WOW! awards

Rather than develop a new stand-alone scheme, the council decided to subscribe to the independent WOW! awards programme – this not only provided external validation but given its cross-sector membership, would make winning awards even more meaningful. The WOW! awards were established to recognize and help improve the standards of customer service in organizations. Their philosophy was encapsulated in the phrase, 'Catching people doing something right'.

Nominations

Only customers can nominate employees for a WOW! award and nominations are validated by the WOW! organization. The model is simple. Posters highlighting the scheme are placed at customer reception points. The main message on the posters is, 'Did we WOW you today? If the service you got from us today was so good that it made you go WOW! – why not nominate us for a WOW Award?'

A simple paper nomination form is available for customers, which when completed they can place in a box provided; alternatively the forms can be sent back by Freepost. Customers can also nominate a member of staff online or by any other method they prefer, including letter, phone and e-mail. The nominations are collated and recorded by the relevant service. All nominees are sent a letter of congratulation. The service (one of the five directorates) sends a list of what they consider to be the best nominations to the corporate team who submit the most exceptional of these to WOW!. WOW! then determine the winners and send certificates back to Haringey for presentation.

Pilot scheme

Officers and councillors were initially wary about introducing such a programme. Therefore, rather than a launch across the whole council, Haringey decided to first run a pilot. The pilot scheme was launched in the registrars and libraries, arts and museum services in June 2006. The success of the pilot exceeded all expectations. Within the first three months, 225 nominations were received – compared with 147 compliments received for the entire council in

2005–6 under the existing compliments scheme. Nominations were attracted not only for the two services in the pilot but others as well. These had been submitted by a wide range of customers too – including children and businesses, and those whose first language is not English. The pilot scheme appeared to have captured the public's imagination.

The overall success of the pilot proved a positive experience all round:

- Customers had a new and quite different opportunity to give feedback on service received.
- Staff felt better and more directly valued.
- Remarkable front-line behaviour that would perhaps have not been brought to the attention of managers and the heads of service was now done so formally.
- The scheme provided very positive publicity for Haringey in both the local and trade press.

WOW! awards launch

Based on the pilot, the WOW! awards scheme was rolled out to customer services in March 2007 and then council-wide in May 2007. The scheme subsumed the existing compliments provisions of the customer feedback scheme, so that any compliments received by any means are counted and included under the WOW! scheme.

The number of customer nominations and winner has been steadily increasing, as can be seen in Table 10.1.

TABLE 10.1   Haringey WOW! awards

Period	Nominations	Winners
Pilot	411	19
2007–8	1,046	49
2008–9	1,176	165
2009–10	1,432	195

What customers said

A council provides some of the most sensitive and vital services to people, some of whom may be in very difficult personal circumstances. Nominations continue to come in from a very wide range of people, some of whom have to go to some personal trouble to put in a nomination. Some examples of the narrative in nominations:

> They don't need to give me the emotional support they give me – but they do it anyway. Always available. Always supportive – thank you.

> Thank you very much for the job you rendered to me this morning. I came to the office with much sorrow, but with your help and direction, healed my wounds. May God richly bless you for your good work. Keep it up.

> I want to praise the above-named staff for their kindness and helpfulness that they extended to me in dealing with a somewhat complicated problem. I am physically disabled, have impaired vision and suffer chronic schizophrenia. In my honest opinion they are a great credit to the London Borough of Haringey. I would be pleased if you would kindly pass on my grateful thanks for their kind, swift and efficient efforts on my behalf.

Celebration

Around 10–15 per cent of those nominated receive a WOW! award; some have won a number, one person has won 11. Approximately every six weeks the latest winners are presented with their awards by a senior councillor at a short ceremony. This is an extract of the speech delivered by one councillor at a recent presentation ceremony:

> We all know how important it is to provide the high-quality services that local people need and deserve. And that, of course, is what the WOW! awards are all about. They give our customers a straightforward non-bureaucratic way to let us know when they have received excellent service. They have proved an inspiration for staff – to keep a clear focus on the needs of those who use our services. And they enable us to celebrate doing a good job – which is very important because working for the council, as we all know, can sometimes be a thankless task. As a councillor too, you generally get to hear about things that have gone wrong, but not too much about what we do well. So the WOW! awards

help keep all of us informed – councillors, directors and managers – where customers have gone out of their way to tell us about the good things.

There is no financial or non-financial award; just the certificates awarded at the ceremony. Other than staff time, the cost is trivial. It is up to the individual what they do with their certificate. Many are hung in the office. Some areas have all the certificates awarded on display on a 'wall of honour'.

Photographs are taken and used in internal publicity promoting what some people have done. From time to time there are also mentions in *People*, Haringey's magazine to all residents.

Impact on other stakeholders

Councillors typically receive complaints from ratepayers or see them to help deal with a problem. Inevitably this gives a negative slant to the activities of those working at Haringey. But the WOW! awards give them a different perspective as it highlights the great things that are going on as recognized by taxpayers.

Similarly, the WOW! awards can give a more balanced view to staff at the council. This can be particularly important where there may be a high-profile problem that may affect one service but can taint the whole council. As one recipient said, 'What a pleasant change it has been to actually be acknowledged for giving a good service to my customers.'

The awards also allow managers to see better what some of their people are doing and how they are perceived by their customers. One manager said, 'As a manager, I thought I knew my staff. The amazing comments we received from customers through the WOW! scheme strengthened and deepened that knowledge. I learnt what it was like to see my staff from the customer's perspective – and that some of the staff I had thought were good are actually excellent.'

Haringey have also won a number of the national awards, such as:

- winners at the National Customer Service Awards 2007, 2008 and 2009;

- 2009 WOW! award winner – best local authority; best team; best healthcare provider as well as a number of finalist positions.

The whole WOW! award approach and these externally validated and awarded national accolades appear to have had a very positive effect on all of the stakeholders: employees, officers, councillors and customers.

KPMG

Background

KPMG in the UK has over 10,000 partners and staff working in 22 offices and is part of a global network of member firms employing over 140,000 people in 146 countries. As part of KPMG Europe it is also part of the largest integrated accounting firm in Europe. KPMG in the UK is a leading provider of professional services, which include audit, tax, and advisory. The majority of employees are graduates.

In the 2009 recession, rather than simply make people redundant, KPMG came up with some innovative ways to help reduce their cost base while giving many of their people in the UK a choice. They allowed people to apply for a sabbatical or reduced working hours. These options were very popular given the circumstances, with over 85 per cent of people across all business areas volunteering to take part. Many other companies followed KPMG's lead to try and find more flexible ways to deal with the need to cut costs while retaining talent.

KPMG has a reward strategy that has underpinned its growth over recent years, focusing on rewarding performance and meeting the needs of its people through a total reward approach. As part of this approach, KPMG operate two main recognition programmes, which are discussed below.

Encore!

Encore! is a peer-recognition programme that was launched in 2002. Anyone can nominate anyone else (other than a partner) in the firm. This can be an individual or team. The programme was launched to recognize and reward those project teams and individuals who have made outstanding contributions to the firm's success, many of whom make personal sacrifices for the greater good of a project and/or the organization. For example, Encore! seeks to:

- celebrate individual and team success;
- recognize exceptional performance;
- reinforce desired and demonstrated behaviours, activities and contributions;
- contribute to establishing a distinct organizational culture.

When launched in 2002, there was an approval form that presented the person nominating with a number of questions to ensure the nominated employee fulfilled the criteria. Every nomination had to be seconded and the line manager had to be either the nominator or the seconder. Final approval of the award was the responsibility of the employee's business unit head, with the costs being attributed to that business unit.

The prize for an individual award was a £250 ($375) Red Letter day voucher and one day off or, instead of the voucher, two days off. The prize for a team award would be a night out or a Red Letter day experience that the whole team could attend.

2006 relaunch

Encore! was relaunched in 2006. Red Letter days were no longer offered and a new e-mail-based nomination and approval process was introduced. Individual awards were typically around £250 (£375) but could be increased by exception. The team awards were usually £1,000 ($1,500) but again this could be varied depending on the numbers in the team and what had been achieved. A rule of thumb for team awards was to aim to award around £100 ($150) per person.

Nominations went to a panel of senior people who considered the nominations made each month. Awards were in the form of vouchers or merchandise through an external provider. Some discretion was available for different business areas within the firm. There were therefore some variations from place to place within KPMG as to how Encore! was used and the values of awards made.

There were also some four or five different local intranet sites that grew up to support the local variation to Encore!

In 2007 there were 1,280 individual awards and 268 team awards made. The total cost represented a minimal percentage of the payroll.

In 2007 a review was undertaken as there had been a number of concerns with the existing system:

- It was relatively time-consuming and expensive in senior manager and partner time to run a monthly panel for relatively small-value awards.
- The size of the awards had been gradually increasing as there was no specified amount given.
- The guideline that 10 per cent of those nominated could receive an award did not seem fair given the range of things for which people were nominated. The likelihood of receiving an award could be influenced by the number and quality of nominations in the month.
- Management information was not readily available from the voucher provider.
- There was considerable manual intervention as the system was not as effective as KPMG wished.
- The recipient's business unit paid for the award, which implied that those in that area made the final decision on awards.
- The local discretion meant that there was inconsistency of application and it was difficult to keep track of the costs of the scheme as a whole.
- There was also a merger of the UK firm with the German and Swiss member firms taking place and KPMG in the UK wanted to establish a single platform.

2008 relaunch

As a result of the review, KPMG in the UK worked with its service provider and made a number of changes to the programme that was relaunched in September 2008:

- The panel ceased to exist.
- A 'Thank you' with no cash value was introduced.

- Specific award levels were introduced.
- An award wizard was introduced to help people select an appropriate level of award.
- Vouchers-only replaced merchandise or vouchers.
- The individual business area discretion was removed and the local intranet sites were taken down.

Awards

The new system has five levels of award ranging from a Thank you e-card only with no cash value to an e-card plus an award of £50, £150, £250 or £1,000 ($75, $225, $375 or $1,500), each with an extra day's holiday. There is also a team award of £150 ($225) per team member plus an extra day's holiday. The awards are in the form of vouchers that can be exchanged at retailers such as John Lewis, BHS, Gap, Waitrose, Halfords, B&Q, Legoland, Marriott International and Amazon.

Award wizard

To provide a framework of consistency, KPMG have developed an online 'Award wizard' to help the nominator find the appropriate level of award. The nominator is asked a series of questions and has to indicate an answer of either Meaningful, Substantial or Extraordinary to each. Example questions are:

- To what degree did the employee find new ways to improve on existing practice, resulting in business impact?
- What degree of business and commercial awareness did the employee display?
- To what degree did the employee exceed your expectations?

Based on the responses, the wizard provides the recommended award level.

Nominations against values

The nomination must fall under one of the following reasons, which are based on KPMG's core values:

- a great win;
- consistently outstanding performance;
- great teamwork;
- knowledge sharing;
- outstanding client service;
- problem solving;
- working across disciplines;
- leadership;
- corporate social responsibility;
- innovation;
- diversity.

Presentations

The nominator sends the person being thanked the e-card via an online system, explaining why they have received the award. Partners and managers are strongly encouraged to publicly recognize and thank those receiving awards, for example at a presentation within a larger group, and it is the manager's/approver's responsibility to make sure this happens. Some awards are also highlighted in local internal newsletters. The recipient will sometimes prefer to keep the news to themselves rather than being put in the spotlight, in which case only the system notification will be used.

What is said

Here are three examples of the thanks expressed on e-cards:

In recognition of exemplary client service and technical skills, we would like to thank you for your dedication and flexibility with the recent project F. Client and member-firm feedback has been outstanding, which has been a great reflection on you and the wider team.

You successfully delivered a major piece of modelling work in half of the allotted time we planned for, due to the client's requirements changing early on in the project. Your attention to detail and sheer drive to get this work completed on time were outstanding.

Thank you for your help over the last year as team leader. You were a pleasure to work with and in my opinion grew immensely as a professional.

Approval

Awards are approved or disapproved in the system, with an automated reminder if no action is taken. The nominator's manager consults with the recipient's manager prior to making a final decision, with the nominator being notified, normally within a few days, either way. The nominator's business unit bears the cost of the award, with the tax and NI liabilities covered by KPMG for both Encore! and the Menu of recognition.

The Menu of recognition

This is an informal scheme that was launched in 2005 for managers to use to recognize their people – primarily support staff. It was to complement Encore! as it had been identified that support staff were rarely recognized in that way. It was believed that this was primarily due to them not doing high-profile client-facing work that was mostly recognized via Encore!

Managers were encouraged to recognize their support staff and use small tangible awards of small gifts, flowers, time off, etc. Its use has subsequently grown so that it may be used for any employee – client facing or support – and when Encore! was reviewed it was retained as a key recognition tool.

KPMG also formally recognize long service with financial 'Landmark awards' at 20, 30 and 40 years. However, the Menu of recognition is recommended to managers to use for shorter service periods, such as 10 years, to recognize an individual. There is no central procurement system; it is for the manager to determine and as appropriate purchase any tangible award. The tax and NI are settled by KPMG. Again, the costs are borne locally by the manager's business area in such a way that the overall costs can be captured and reported on.

A culture of recognition

Education around reward and recognition, including the online platform, are covered in manager training and coaching programmes that help effective management of the schemes. KPMG's approach to reward and recognition is also explained on the induction course, so from day one new joiners are aware of the culture of recognizing and rewarding outstanding contribution.

There is no formal link between the recognition programmes and the firm's formal performance management system. However, an individual or their manager are encouraged to bring the fact that they received a recognition award into the discussion about their performance over the year.

How is the impact of recognition measured?

KPMG regularly reviews its recognition schemes and continues to strive to improve them. Management information relating to the scheme is reviewed and shared with the business every quarter, with a full annual review.

KPMG run an engagement survey every two years to understand employees' perceptions better. This covers a number of aspects of employment with KPMG. Two statements are included that refer to recognition, to which participants are asked to show their level of agreement:

- KPMG makes adequate use of recognition and rewards other than money to encourage good performance.
- How satisfied are you with the recognition you receive for your performance?

The positive responses to both have increased significantly from 2005 to 2008.

KPMG also benchmarks itself externally as an employer of choice, and over the past six years has consistently been placed in the top 10 in the Sunday Times Best Big Companies to Work For list. While there may be a less direct link than from the engagement survey, KPMG's approach to recognition may well have contributed to this position.

Prudential

Background

Established in 1848, Prudential employ over 27,000 people world-wide and have over 21 million customers with around £250 billion ($375 billion) funds under management. The group is structured around four main business units including Prudential UK and Europe.

Prudential UK is a leading life and pensions provider with approximately 7 million customers in the UK. Employing approximately 2,800 people, it operates from two core strategic UK sites in Stirling and Reading and has offices in London and Dublin, as well as a customer service centre in Mumbai.

Prudential UK provides a range of products and services including individual and bulk annuities, individual and corporate pensions, with-profits bonds, onshore and offshore bonds, savings and investments, healthcare and protection products. Prudential is also the corporate pension provider to 20 per cent of FTSE 350 companies and manages more than 4,000 pension schemes.

These products are offered to customers through a number of distribution channels including financial advisers, business-to-business (consulting actuaries and benefit advisers), partnerships (affinities and banks) and direct-to-customers (telephone, internet and mail).

Behaviours

In July 2006 a number of changes were initiated including a new more flexible Performance Management system and a new bonus arrangement. At the centre of the changes was the development of four behaviours.

These were developed as part of a project which used the Human Synergistics International Organizational Culture Inventory (OCI) Survey. Human Synergistics International state that 'The OCI provides a picture of an organization's operating culture in terms of the behaviours that members believe are expected or implicitly required. By guiding the way in which members approach their work and interact with one another, these "behavioural norms" determine the organization's capacity to solve problems, adapt to change, and perform effectively.'

The four behaviours that were derived from the survey and associated consultancy work are:

- deliver;
- inspire;
- challenge;
- connect.

New recognition programme

Prudential had various local recognition schemes operating in different parts of the business. They had grown up over time and were used in different ways to recognize different things. As part of the change it was decided to bring in a more consistent approach to recognition that would reinforce the four behaviours. The new programme would replace the various locally managed recognition schemes. The change was implemented in April 2009.

The new scheme, called simply 'Recognition', was 'designed to acknowledge people who have demonstrated excellence in at least one of our four behaviours and gone beyond what's expected in their role'. Prudential UK believed that by re-energizing how they recognize this type of achievement they could hope to inspire more people to achieve these levels of excellence and build a culture that supports a high-performing organization.

Manager guidance

As part of the launch, Prudential gave some guidelines to managers to position the new scheme:

> Recognition is not part of the performance management, salary review and bonus process. It enables you to recognize people for specific instances where they have demonstrated actions that are above and beyond what is expected of them and that support our four behaviours. It is also worth remembering that the simplest and often most powerful way to recognize someone is by saying 'Thank you and well done' personally and quickly. Recognition will make it easy for you to do this.

Three tiers

Nominations may be made via the online portal within or across teams, functions and business areas. Anyone can nominate an individual for an award. People managers can also nominate groups of people. Nominations may be made for one of three tiers:

- Tier one: A non-financial simple 'thank you' in the form of an e-card;
- Tier two: A 'thank you' e-card plus a financial award of £25, £50, £75 or £100 ($38, $75, $113 or $150);
- Tier three: A 'thank you' e-card plus a quarterly financial award for a team or individual for each of the four behaviours. For individuals, the awards are up to £500 ($750) and up to £250 ($375) for the runner-up. For teams; up to £1,000 ($1,500) for a team winner and up to £500 ($750) for the team runner-up. Winners and runners-up for these quarterly awards are decided from the tier-three nominations made for the quarter by a panel of representatives from around the business.

The portal is hosted and run by an external third-party provider. Winners of an award can log into the portal and redeem the award for a large variety of products, shopping vouchers, experience days or charitable gifts. The majority of winners redeem their vouchers through the retail section of major retailers such as Sainsbury's, John Lewis, Marks & Spencer, Debenhams, Currys. Other sections that are also used include travel and entertainment. The company settles the tax liability via the PSA.

What is said

Here are three examples of some of the messages of thanks given to people:

> Wanted to say thank you to Anne for covering late cover tonight at very short notice. This is great from a teamwork point of view and very flexible of Anne.

> I would like to say a huge thank you for your continued hard work and support on the sales process pilot. You have continued to deliver on this project and your weekly updates have been excellent.

For your continued hard work and support with the customer champion programme. You are very proactive and are inspiring your colleagues to think about the customer in everything they do. Well done!

Approvals

For a tier-three award a form has to be completed under the following headings, in addition to basic information such as name, business unit, etc:

- Behaviour.
- Reason.
- Tell us what your nominee(s) did.
- Tell us why this is exceptional/above and beyond their normal role(s).
- Tell us what impact this had.
- Tell us how this has supported us in our aim of becoming leaders in retirement.
- Tell us about any feedback that has been received from others.
- Any further comments.
- Recognition award already given?

Here is a summarized example of what someone was nominated for and awarded a tier-three award:

Identified that approx 35 per cent of daily e-mail requests received contained incomplete information. The data provided by the partner was insufficient to produce a non-standard pre-sale illustration by return. Instead we had to e-mail to ask for the additional information to allow us to produce the illustration. John designed a document that incorporated all the product types that could possibly be requested, and designed it in such a way that when any particular product was selected, then only the fields and options for that product would be returned for completion. This in turn meant that all required information would be completed, and we could produce the illustration without further delay. John used his initiative to suggest a much more structured approach than just reminding partners to provide the correct information. He recognized a more significant change in process was required, and was able to put across his ideas to a senior manager. He had no previous experience of this type of approach, and looked to me for guidance if there were any difficult issues. We've seen a gradual use of the form, and currently 10 per cent of new requests use the form. He has taken time to train his colleagues and provide a full understanding of the form, so anyone can answer queries if they arise. His ideas and willingness to find better ways of working and come up with solutions are some of the key qualities we want to see and encourage in our staff. He has already received many recognition awards, reflecting the time and effort he puts in for others in the admin centre.

A tier-one e-card must be approved by the line manager of the person nominated. For the tier-two financial award, the manager of the nominator's own business unit must also approve the financial award. It was felt important that there was an approval to try to get some consistency and ensure, as far as possible, that the nomination was reasonable against the criteria. It was also important as the cost of tier-two awards is borne by the nominator's cost centre and is charged against the allocated recognition budget.

Reviews

Prudential review the activity within the scheme quarterly with a recognition panel. Each quarter they consider how if at all they may wish to change some aspect of the arrangement. For example, how to use examples of the things people have done to be nominated, changing the communications and reviewing the approval process.

In the first year, over 3,000 awards were made, of which 85 per cent were tier one, 14 per cent were tier two and 1 per cent were tier three. With a total population of 2,800, this is very high usage, suggesting that people have engaged well with the scheme.

Perhaps not surprisingly, the behaviour most recognized was 'deliver' (56 per cent) and the least recognized was 'challenge' (6 per cent). To try to help people understand what the behaviours actually looked like in action, Prudential give examples of the behaviours from the recognition scheme in their in-house magazine.

Prudential believed that the word 'deliver' as one of the four behaviours was too narrow and implied something mainly transactional, representing only *what* was done. They changed from 'deliver' to 'achieve' from April 2010 to try to make the behaviour broader and try to reflect something of the *how* something was done.

Using the data

Prudential provide the usage numbers and other relevant data to the relevant HR business partners. They are then able to use the data in their discussions as they work with the business in whatever way is most appropriate. Different areas in the business use the data to greater and less extents. The operations area has really embedded the recognition scheme; it sits at the centre of what they are trying to do from a cultural perspective. For example, they have team meetings and conferences where recognition winners are called up on stage. They are also the biggest users of management information and use it to identify behavioural themes.

Recognition links

While there is not a formal link with the performance management system, Prudential expect that recognition awards may be brought up in review discussions by the manager or individual. Prudential have two ratings in their annual review, one for the what and one for the how. They are brought together to provide a rating that impacts the bonus that someone might receive. A recognition award may indirectly influence the annual rating and hence bonus.

British Sky Broadcasting Group plc

Background

Sky is the UK's leading entertainment and communications company, providing pay TV broadband and telephony services to almost 10 million homes. Sky has continually innovated in technology, being the first in the UK to launch digital TV in 1998, Sky+ in 2001, Sky+HD in 2006 and 3D TV in 2010. Sky became the world's first carbon-neutral media company in 2006. Sky employ some 16,000 people in 15 locations in the UK.

Recognition in Sky

Sky operates both a corporate high-profile recognition scheme and a number of locally run schemes. Divisions are free to develop their own recognition schemes within overall guidelines to reflect their own culture. A single online platform, run by an external third-party specialist provider, is used to deliver awards across the business.

Sky had an informal approach to recognition in some divisions for many years. In 2005, the company focused on recognition, to better use it as a lever to drive engagement and also in response to employee feedback. This led to the introduction of the company-wide 'Team Sky' programme in 2005. This programme reflected the company's brand and entertainment values, using imagery of comic heroes to encourage people all across Sky to recognize their colleagues. The approach to recognition in each business area was also reviewed and led to the development of more structured programmes themed to each area.

Since then, the regular people survey has included a set of questions that track people's perceptions about recognition at divisional and overall company levels. These recognition scores are a major indicator used to shape the development of both divisional schemes and the company-wide plan. The recognition scores have continued to move up. Over the years, the Team Sky concept has been extremely successful. The corporate and main divisional programmes are described below.

Team Sky

The Team Sky awards is a Sky-wide programme that is designed to reinforce Sky culture, Sky values and create role models. During 2008 there was a four-week window for people to nominate any individual or any team, to recognize their contribution over 2008, with the awards being presented in early 2009. There were around 2,000 individual nominations and over 300 team nominations.

HR managers in each division took the lead in sifting individual and team nominations into excellent, good and weak categories, and set up local judging panels with senior management. All 'good' nominations were sent a letter from Sky's director of people together with a desk plaque, while the 'excellent' nominations went to the divisional panel for closer review, and each division eventually chose 5–10 nominations to forward to the final executive panel.

At each stage, the nominations were examined against the overall criterion of 'Believe in better' (externally, this is the Sky advert strapline, and internally it is the prime business value), looking for actual examples of what individuals had done and how teams had collaborated with other departments.

Finally, the executive panel judged the final shortlist and awarded the prizes to the overall Sky winners at the different levels:

Individuals:
- Level 1: five winners; five-day trip for two to South Africa;
- Level 2: five winners; dinner for two at the Eiffel Tower/in Salzburg/in London;
- Level 3: 10 winners; Sony HD console.

Team: six winners; choice of team experience/movie night/ football match.
Team Sky 'S' (plaque for home or desk) for all high-quality nominations.

For the Level 1 winners, the CEO organized a surprise 'drop-in' visit for each of them at a regular or specially arranged team meeting. Profiles of each winner were prepared with information on their history at Sky and the background to their nomination and award; the CEO used this to congratulate the winner when presenting the prize.

For Level 2 and 3 winners, the appropriate divisional executive 'dropped-in' to congratulate the winners and present the prizes.

Divisional recognition

Local recognition programmes tailored to each business area also operate across Sky. These plans work to a common set of principles and parameters and are themed and managed in a way to reflect the culture and priorities of the unit. Three of these local recognition programmes are outlined below.

GRAFTA (Grand recognition award for tremendous achievement)

This scheme was developed within and for the Entertainment group, which commissions drama and comedy content; hence the play on the name from BAFTA. This is a monthly employee recognition scheme that rewards employees for going above and beyond the duties of their role. The 400 staff in Entertainment can, however, nominate anyone across Sky.

Employee nominations are submitted by e-mail or through the GRAFTA intranet page during the first two weeks of each month. A different promotional poster campaign each month uses adaptations of well-known films. Nominations are reviewed by a panel consisting of the heads of department, the HR manager and the employee forum representative.

The prizes are a gold paperweight star, £250 ($375) retail vouchers and a GRAFTA certificate in a gold envelope – normally presented by the head of entertainment at a team meeting or other suitable event to ensure public recognition. A communication is sent out to everyone in Entertainment announcing the winner, the reasons they won, and including a list of people who were nominated. Details of the winners are placed on the GRAFTA intranet site, which provides everyone with the winners' details, what was said about them and a publicity shot.

Goldenballs

This scheme is run for the 600 employees within Sky Sports. Goldenballs is a monthly employee recognition scheme designed to reward those who make an outstanding contribution towards the continued success of Sky Sports.

Anyone can make a nomination, and all nominations are reviewed by a panel consisting of senior managers and chaired by the HR manager.

There are four winners who each receive a trophy (a Newton's cradle with golden balls) and £300 ($450) of vouchers. The awards are presented by the head of Sky Sports, with monthly e-mails sent out to all staff, advising of winners and nominees. A photo-board with pictures of all the winners is displayed in the main area of Sky Sports.

FAME

For 5,000 customer advisors in Sky's contact centres a different format is adopted. Rather than monthly nomination and review, any employee can send an e-Fame card at any time. Sky FAME is all about on-the-spot recognition for people who do a great job every day, and has the ability to recognize anyone at any time.

This peer-to-peer scheme allows an advisor to instantly recognize colleagues in one of the designated FAME categories:

● Team guru – the one people turn to;
● Hidden gem – unnoticed, but goes the extra mile;
● Life and soul – big personality with a sense of camaraderie;
● Shining example – something truly amazing.

Additionally, nominators can request that small gifts are awarded, ranging from badges to FAME-branded sports holdalls.

Nominations for 'VIP – good at everything and sets the standards' – are made through heads of department, with quarterly awards, including personal letters from the head of the contact centres, and vouchers for restaurants or retail chains.

Finally, there is an annual FAME dinner with the ceremony giving extra recognition to the 'Best of the best' advisor in each of the FAME categories, and extra recognition to the 20 people who have continually delivered excellent customer satisfaction.

The administration system

Nominations are made in different ways in the divisional schemes and winners are also selected using different mechanisms. Behind the scenes, a common admin system ensures efficiency and consistency. The system is managed by designated administrators in each area. They may be the PA to the director or hold a divisional role that enables them to act as a focal point for the division's plan.

They process the division's awards on the system, including personalized messages written by the nominator or the selection panel. The recipient receives an e-mail showing the message and also giving logon details, and they can then access the central recognition website. Here they can choose which brand of vouchers to take from a wide variety of retailers. The third-party provider then sends the vouchers to the employee.

The single third-party provider online platform was introduced in 2006. Using one central point allows Sky to know what recognition is taking place, to be able to review consistency and trends, and to provide a simple system for nomination, receipt and, finally, redemption of the award. Also, with monthly reporting from their provider, it enables Sky to allocate costs to the nominating divisions, and to be clear on its tax liability. Sky settles the tax due on all the awards via their PSA.

Recognition tips

Sky have developed a range of tips and advice on how to manage recognition, which can be viewed by all employees on the internal website, but is particularly useful for new managers.

Four elements

Everyone wants to do a good job for their customers and their colleagues and wants to enjoy what they are doing. Everyone needs to be acknowledged and valued for their contributions, especially if they do something outstanding.

The key to effective recognition is to understand that recognition comes in many forms. Here are four key elements of recognition that really work:

- Praise:
  - Keep it in proportion: don't go over the top, yet don't underplay it.
  - Do it at the right time: don't wait; the sooner the better.
  - Clear and simple: don't ramble, tell them what they did and what you appreciated about it.

- Thanks:
  - Say thanks: that's what it's all about.
  - Be sincere: say it like you mean it and find the right time to do it.
  - Think about how you deliver it and vary from time to time eg in person, via e-mail.
- Opportunity:
  - Constantly look for opportunities to recognize people: there's potential with every interaction eg e-mails, feedback, team meetings, delegating, 1-2-1s.
  - Also provide people with new opportunities: to contribute in new ways, learn new skills, to have more freedom in how they approach work.
- Respect:
  - Recognize people not just for what they do but who they are.
  - Consider employee needs as you make decisions and you recognize employee value.

One size doesn't fit all

One of the most important things to remember with recognition is that one size does not fit all! As you know, what will truly engage one person may switch off another. By operating mass recognition with no appreciation of the individual needs and interests of your employees, at best they'll feel half acknowledged!

Some people like public recognition; others prefer a private thank you. Some like to engage in corporate schemes like Team Sky; others prefer things on a more informal basis. So keep things fresh and continually review what you do.

Key tips for individual recognition

- Identify how each individual contributes.
- Learn more about people around you and what's important to them.
- Recognize unique contributions with personalized recognition that takes interests into account.

What some great managers do

- Great managers make recognition part of their day-to-day approach to leadership! They find ways to add employee recognition to every interaction.
- When you delegate, add a little praise.
- When you receive updates from your team, thank them for being so prompt, thorough or accurate.
- When you hold a team meeting talking about a new challenge, express confidence in your team's ability to meet that challenge.

Some techniques of great managers we found

I ensure I say good morning to every single person in the team – really simple but creates a more positive environment.

I send a handwritten note to each direct report on the anniversary of their hire date – thanking them for their contribution and picking out key achievements.

I go to each member of the team at the end of the day and find out what went well for them that day.

Occasionally I'll ask a more senior manager to send a letter of acknowledgment to those that have made a significant contribution in my team.

I sometimes take time to stop and think about each member of my team in turn and when I last recognized them – then take action as required.

I make a conscious effort to ask for feedback as often as I can – I get some great insights and people appreciate getting a chance to air their views.

Don't get caught out with some common recognition myths

- Some people believe being paid is the only recognition that people need.
- Some managers believe that recognition takes us too much time.
- Some managers believe if they do too much recognition they'll be accused of playing favourites.

Standard Chartered Bank plc

Background

Standard Chartered is a major global bank, formed in 1969 through a merger of two banks: The Standard Bank of British South Africa, founded in 1863, and the Chartered Bank of India, Australia and China, founded in 1853. The bank now employs over 75,000 people worldwide, representing 125 nationalities. Standard Chartered has a network of over 1,600 branches and outlets in more than 70 countries and earns more than 90 per cent of its operating income and profits in Asia, Africa and the Middle East.

Standard Chartered's commitment to customers and its employees is stated as:

- Customers: passionate about our customers' success, delighting them with the quality of our service;
- Our people: helping our people to grow, enabling individuals to make a difference and teams to win.

Core values

To deliver on these commitments, the bank has identified five core values to drive the behaviours of staff:

- courageous;
- responsive;
- international;
- creative;
- trustworthy.

The values are a central element of the way things are done at Standard Chartered and are embedded in its performance management processes. Many organizations try to reflect both the 'what' and the 'how' of performance as part of their performance management system. Recognizing the criticality of behaviours as part of engagement and business performance, Standard Chartered has systematically embedded this duality into its performance management process by using two ratings in the annual performance appraisal. There is a numeric rating (1–5) for performance against objectives, and an alphabetic rating (A–D) for demonstrating the company values.

This process brings to life the importance of living the values at Standard Chartered. Managers and employees agree at the beginning of the year their values objective. During the year, managers and peers are asked for feedback on how their colleagues are exemplifying the behaviours they committed to. At the performance evaluation, reflected in the two ratings, the 'how' in terms of behaviours is considered as much as the 'what' in terms of outcomes and both have an influence on final reward conversations.

Engagement survey

Clearly, there is a strong link between the values, desired culture and behaviours and the level of engagement of people in the bank. If the values, culture and behaviours are 'right' then you might reasonably expect to see this reflected in the level of engagement. The bank sees measuring levels of engagement as a vital element of the whole as they recognize the business imperative of high employee engagement. So for some years the bank has undertaken an annual staff engagement survey using the Gallup Q12 as the core, with some bespoke questions. One of these Q12 statements to which participants are asked to respond is, 'In the last seven days I have received recognition or praise for doing good work' (see Chapter 2). The bank is able to analyse the results down to the team level so business leaders can see how engaged people are and what impact their manager appears to have. The results from this survey are taken very seriously by the leadership at Standard Chartered, and are taken into account not just in the performance appraisal system but in development, succession planning and promotion decisions.

Impact of engagement

The bank has leveraged the wealth of data available from the engagement survey to understand the drivers of engagement within the organization, and validate the performance benefits. This has led them to understand the pivotal role played by managers in influencing employee engagement through their behaviours. The bank found that branches with a statistically significant increase in levels of employee engagement had a 16 per cent higher profit margin growth than branches with decreased levels of employee engagement. They also identified that the biggest impact on the levels of engagement was the manager. They therefore place a very strong focus on the importance of the relationship between the manager and individual.

Role of managers

The bank has identified through internal research four principles that are exhibited by managers of highly engaged employees:

- Know me
  - Take time to understand my talents and strengths – what I do best.
- Focus me
  - Help me get really clear on what excellence looks like.
  - Help me achieve excellence by doing what I do best.
  - Constantly let me know how I'm doing and help me stay on track.
- Care about me
  - Get to know me as a person and make me feel valued for who I am.
- Inspire me
  - Help me understand my significance in the bank's mission.
  - Create conditions for team working and a fun environment.

Standard Chartered take management development and training very seriously. In all management development programmes, recognition is embedded as part of what is seen as being an effective manager in the bank. For example, 'The great manager' programme is for newly appointed managers and has both online tools and in-person sessions. The programme concentrates on the behaviours and skills that are needed to be a great manager at Standard Chartered.

Managers are encouraged to treat every interaction with their staff as an opportunity to have a coaching discussion to give praise and recognize a job well done, give constructive feedback on areas requiring more work, or discuss what help and support might be needed to carry out the job. The bank believes that managers need to use timely, regular, appropriate recognition or praise as it is a vital element of the overall level of engagement. It is possible to offer awards such as a small gift or dinner out, but the local line managers have a high degree of freedom to decide what will work best for individuals. This is part of the emphasis on knowing your people. Standard Chartered believe that as a result staff are better focused, motivated and engaged, which is reflected in improved business outcomes – lower staff turnover and improved financial performance.

Decentralized approach

Standard Chartered will normally take a 'one bank' approach to HR policies and programmes in order to support its culture and provide globally consistent, cost-effective, streamlined global processes. However, when it comes to recognition, they believe that it needs to be driven locally to adapt to business requirements and specific individual needs. So even where there are slightly more formal recognition programmes in the bank, they are country or locally based.

References

By individual authors

Armstrong, M (1996) *Employee Reward*, IPD, London

Blanchard, K and Johnson, S (1993) *The One Minute Manager*, HarperCollins, London

Boyle, D C (1995) *Secrets of a Successful Employee Recognition System*, Productivity Press, Portland, Oregon

Bryant, S (1994) 'Say it with flowers', *Human Resources*, Summer, pp 120–5

Buckingham, M and Coffman, C (1999) *First, Break all the Rules*, Simon & Schuster, New York

Carnegie, D (1936) *How to Win Friends and Influence People*, Simon and Schuster, New York

Caudron, S (1995) 'The top 20 ways to motivate employees', *Industry Week*, 3 April, **244** (7)

Churchill, W (1944) *Hansard*, volume 398, cc 872–1002, speech to House of Commons, 22 March

Conference Board Inc (1992) 'Recognizing quality achievement: non-cash award programs', report no 1008

Deci, E L (1975) *Intrinsic Motivation*, Plenum Press, New York

Fisher, J (2005) *How to Run Successful Employee Incentive Schemes*, Kogan Page, London

Flannery, T P, Hofrichter, D A and Platten, P E (1996) *People, Performance and Pay*, The Free Press, New York

Freiberg, K and Freiberg, J (1996) *Nuts! Southwest Airlines' Crazy Recipe for Business and Personal Success*, Bard Press, Austin, TX

Friedson, A S (1985) 'Special award programs: compensating excellence', *Personnel Administrator*, September, pp 105–14

Gostick, A and Elton, C (2007) *The Carrot Principle*, Free Press, New York

Gryna, D (1992) 'Celebrating success', *Managing Service Quality*, September, pp 329–33

Hale, R E and Maehling, R F (1993) *Recognition Redefined*, Monochrome Press, Exeter, New Hampshire

Harvey-Jones, J (1994) *All Together Now*, Heinemann, London

Hemsath, D and Yerkes, L (1997) *301 Ways to Have Fun at Work*, Berrett-Koehler, San Francisco

Herzberg, F (1968) *Work and the Nature of Man*, Granada, London

Herzberg, F, Mausner, B and Snyderman, B B (1959) *The Motivation to Work*, John Wiley & Sons, New York

Jeffrey, S (2003) 'The benefits of tangible non-monetary incentives', Executive White Paper, The SITE Foundation

Jeffrey, S (2004) *Right Answer, Wrong Question*, University of Chicago

Jeffries, R (1997) 'Reaping the rewards of recognition', *HR Focus*, January, **74** (1), p 9

Johnson, R and Redmond, D (1998) *The Art of Empowerment*, Financial Times Pitman Publishing, London

Joinson, C (1996) 'Reward your best employees', *HR Magazine*, April, pp 49–55

Juran, J (2003) *Juran on Leadership For Quality*, Simon & Schuster, New York

Kerr, S (1997) *Ultimate Rewards*, HBS Press, Boston

Klubnik, J P (1995) *Rewarding and Recognising Employees*, Irwin, New York

Kohn, A (1993) 'Why incentive plans cannot work', *Harvard Business Review*, September–October

Kouzes, J M and Posner, B Z (2007) *The Leadership Challenge*, Jossey-Bass, San Francisco

La Motta, T (1995) *Recognition The Quality Way*, Quality Resources, New York

Lyons, L (2000) 'Management is dead...', *People Management*, 26 October, pp 60–4

Machiavelli, N (1961) *The Prince*, PenguinClassics, London

MacLeod, D and Clark, N (2009) 'Engaging for success: enhancing performance through employee engagement: A report to government

Maslow, A H (1970) *Motivation and Personality*, Harper & Row, New York

Maynard, R (1997) 'How to motivate low-wage workers', *Nation's Business*, May

Nelson, B (1994) *1001 Ways to Reward Employees*, Workman Publishing, New York

Nelson, B (1996) 'Dump the cash, load on the praise', *Personnel Journal*, July, pp 65–70

Nelson, B (2003) *The 1001 Rewards & Recognition Fieldbook*, Workman Publishing, New York

Pink, D (2009) 'Dan Pink on the surprising science of motivation': www.ted.com/talks/dan_pink_on_motivation.html

Pfeffer, J and Sutton, R I (2006) *Hard Facts, Dangerous Half-Truths and Total Nonsense*, Harvard Business School Press, Boston

Pitts, C (1995) *Motivating Your Organisation*, McGraw-Hill, Maidenhead

Rath, T and Clifton, D O (2004) *How Full Is Your Bucket?*, Gallup Press, New York

Rose, M (2001) *Recognising Performance*, CIPD, London

Rucci, A J et al (1998) 'The employee–customer–profit chain at Sears', Harvard Business Review, January–February, pp 82–97

Skinner, B F (1953) Science and Human Behavior, Macmillan, New York

Stajkovic, A D and Luthans, F (1997) 'A meta-analysis of the effects of organisational behavior modification on task performance, 1975–95', Academy of Management Journal, **40**, pp 1122–49

Steers, R M and Porter, L W (1991) Motivation and Work Behavior, McGraw-Hill, New York

Syedain, H (1995) 'The rewards of recognition', Management Today, May, pp 72–4

Truss, C, Soane, E, Edwards, C, Wisdom, K, Croll, A and Burnett, J. (2006) Working Life: Employee Attitudes and Engagement, CIPD, London

Tulgan, B (1996) Managing Generation X, Capstone, Oxford

Tyson, S (1995) Human Resource Strategy, Pitman, London

Vroom, V H (1964) Work and Motivation, Willey, New York

Wagner, R and Harter, J K (2006) 12: The Elements of Great Managing, Gallup Press, New York

Yeomans, J and Arnold, C (2006) Teaching Learning and Psychology, David Fulton Press, London

Other

'Absence Management Annual Survey Report' (2009) CIPD

'Benefits to make staff happy' (2007) Employee Benefits, October, pp 53–6

'Create a strategy that earns respect' (2008) Employee Benefits, motivation supplement, September, pp 3–4

'Leveraging recognition: non-cash incentives to improve performance' (2006) Workspan, November, pp 19–22

'MGM Grand: how employee recognition impacts the bottom line' (2008) Workspan, August, pp 52–5

'Recognition pays' (2005) Discovery White Paper, O C Tanner Company

'Reward and recognition program profiles and best practices' (2009) The Ascent Group Inc

'The hard facts' (2008) Personnel Today, September, pp 26–9

'The management agenda' (2007) Roffey Park Management Institute

'The state of human resources' (2010) King's College London

'The value and ROI in employee recognition' (2009) Human Capital Institute

'Trends in pay and benefits systems' (1995) CBI/Hay

Index

NB: page numbers in *italic* indicate figures or tables

100 Club   33, 38, 87
3
     case study   128–33
          3Cheers   131
          annual staff survey   132
          business overview   128
          Fearless programme   132–33
          focus workshops   132
          Just rewards   129
          Oscars@3   65, 131
          Round of applause   65, 76, 130–31
          team performance health check
               (TPHC)   133
          thank you cards   65, 128–29
     and management training   106
     and third-party providers   79

absenteeism   120–21
action plan   125
Amazon   163
armed forces, recognition in   28–29
Armstrong, Michael   48
Ascent Group survey   87

B&Q   163
Best 600 Companies to Work For   3–4
BHS   163
Blanchard, Ken and Johnson, Spencer
          43, 49
Boyle, Daniel   33, 85–86
Bright Sparks   *see* Comet Group plc
British Airways   74, 100
British Sky Broadcasting Group plc
     case study   172–79
          annual survey   173
          business overview   172
          FAME   176
          Goldenballs   175–76
          GRAFTA   175
          local recognition programmes   174
          nomination system   176–77
          recognition tips   177–78
          Team Sky   173–74

and guidelines   33
and local programmes   74
and programme name   76
and third-party providers   79
'broadbanding'   104

Cabinet Office   27
Carnegie, Andrew   16
Carnegie, Dale   16–17
cash, using
     definition   2
     immediate awards   57–58
     levels of awards   58
     and the payslip   57
Chartered Institute of Personnel and
          Development (CIPD) reward
          survey   2–4, *3, 4*
Churchill, Winston   29
Colley, Stephen   123
Comet Group plc
     case study   137–44
          annual employee survey   143–44
          appraisals   144
          Bright Sparks   39, 142–43
          business overview   137
          Comet stars   139–40
          manager recognition toolkit   77,
               140–41
          Millionaires' Club   114, 141–42
          recognition dos and don'ts   143
          store manager of the year   114,
               142
          thank you cards   138–39
     Comet Life   139, 140, 143
     and guidelines   33
     and long service   37
     and management training   106
     and recognition by customers   34
     and social reinforcement   113–14
     and supporting managers   50
Conference and Incentive Travel magazine
          poll   116
Conference Board Inc survey   90

Conspicuous Gallantry Cross   28
Co-operative Group, The   69
Currys   169
customers
    incentivizing   121
    recognition by   53–54

Debenhams   169
demotivation   5
Department for Business, Enterprise and
        Regulatory Reform (BERR)   133
Department for Business, Innovation and
        Skills (BIS)
    case study   133–37
        annual survey   133–34
        business overview   133
        corporate centre awards   134
        corporate values   134
        Hilary's awards   134
        in-year bonus   136
        management groups   133
        performance management
            system   136–37
        permanent secretary's award   135
        special awards   135–36
    and team awards   46
Department for Innovation, Universities
        and Skills (DIUS)   133
differentiation   8–9
Douglas, Hilary   134
Driver and Vehicle Licensing Agency   121

Edexcel
    case study   144–48
        business overview   144–45
        performance management
            system   148
        Star cards   65, 145–46
        Star exceptional awards   65,
            147–48
        Star value awards   34, 65, 146–47
    and management training   106
    and programme name   76
    RoundUp   146
Einstein, Albert   38, 109
employee development   104–06, 105
    role of line managers   106
Encore! Programme   see KPMG
encouragement award   96, 97
engagement   22–24
    disengagement   26–27
    Gallup Q12   24, 87, 181
    and human resources
    key jobs   30
    MacLeod report   23
    Sears Roebuck study   23

at Standard Chartered Bank   23
State of Human Resources Survey   24
YouGov People Index   23–24
evaluability   11
expectancy theory   112–13
extrinsic motivation   17

Facebook   129, 151
FAME   see British Sky Broadcasting
        Group plc
Fearless programme   see 3 financial
        benefit awards   96–97
Friedson, A S   86, 91
Furnham, Adrian   7, 100, 110

Gallup   21, 23, 48, 72–73
    Q12   24, 87, 181
Gap   163
Generation Y   45
Glucksberg, Sam   110–11
Goldenballs   see British Sky Broadcasting
        Group plc
'golf club effect'   69–70
Gracian, Baltasar   7
GRAFTA   see British Sky Broadcasting
        Group plc
Great Ormond Street Hospital (GOSH)
    case study   149–54
        appraisals   154
        business overview   149
        ceremony   152–53
        nomination categories   150–51
        nomination procedure   151–52
        performance management
            system   154
        reception   154
        recognition programmes
            history   149–50
    and celebration   56
    and language   64
    and recognition by customers   34, 54
Greene King plc   34

Halfords   163
happiness   26
Haringey Council
    case study   155–60
        business overview   155
        customer feedback   158
        customer service   155
        effect on stakeholders   159–60
        WOW! award nominations   155–56
        WOW! ceremony   158–59
        WOW! launch   157
        WOW! pilot scheme   156–57
    and celebration   56–57

and monitoring programme usage 71
and recognition by customers 34, 54
Harvey-Jones, Sir John 52, 55, 57–58
Herzberg, Frederick 17–18, 44, 46, 47, 50,
    63, 76, 101, 104
  hygiene factors 18
  motivators 18
highly-paid employees, rewarding 61–62
Hilary's awards see Department for
    Business, Innovation and Skills
    (BIS)
HM Revenue and Customs (HMRC) 36,
    38, 136, 143
How to Win Friends and Influence
    People 16
HRM Singapore 47
Human Synergistics International
  Organizational Culture Inventory (OCI)
    Survey 167–68
Hurlock, Dr Elizabeth 22
Hutchison Whampoa Limited 128

ICI 52
incentive plans
  and absenteeism 120–21
  definition of 1, 2
  incentives and focus 110–11
  incentives and motivation 109–12
  incentivizing customers 121
  key jobs
  non-cash incentive plans 116–20
  time span 114–15
  vs recognition programmes 31–32, 32,
    101–02
International Survey Research 25
intrinsic motivation 17
Irwell Valley Housing Association 121

Jackson Organization, The 89, 90
Jeffrey, Scott 7–8
Jeffries, Rosalind 45
John Lewis 146, 163, 169
Johnson, Ron and Redmond, David 48
Juran, Joseph 100
Just rewards see 3
justifiability 11

Kanter, Rosabeth Moss 63, 85, 100
KESA 137
Kohn, Alfie 111
Kouzes, Jim and Posner, Barry 49, 51
KPMG
  case study 160–66
    awards 163
    business overview 160
    core values 164

Encore! programme 2002–
    06 160–61
Encore! programme 2006–
    08 161–62
Encore! programme 2008–
    now 76, 162–63
  engagement survey 166
  Landmark awards 165
  menu of recognition 44, 165
  performance management
    system 166
  presentations 164
  and guidelines 32–33
  and management training 106
  and team awards 46
  and third-party providers 79

La Motta 86
language, use of 64
Lawler, Ed 31, 90
Legoland 163
Lewin, Curt 16
Liverpool fire service 120–21
Loch Fyne 34
long service awards 36, 97
Lyons, L 49

Machiavelli, Niccolò 16, 99
MacLeod report 23, 48
Management Agenda, The 25
managers, recognition by 48–53
  and empowerment 50
  Gallup research 48–49
  how to do it 51–53
  impact of 49–50, 50
  individualizing recognition 52
  as a leadership skill 49
  support for managers 50–51
Marks & Spencer 169
Marriott International 163
Mary Kay Cosmetics 62
Maslow, Abraham 19–20, 47, 113, 114
  esteem need 20
  hierarchy of needs 19, 19
McCormick, Ernest and Ilgen, Daniel 49
McNamara, Robert 1
memory value 9–10, 10
menu of recognition see KPMG
Mercer, William M 102
Metropolitan Police, The 37, 55–56, 59
MGM Grand 89
Millionaires' Club see Comet Group plc
MORI 132
Mother Teresa 15
motivation theory
  expectancy theory 112–13

extrinsic motivation   17
Herzberg, Frederick   17–19
   hygiene factors   18
   motivators   18
intrinsic motivation   17
key jobs   30
Maslow, Abraham
   esteem need   20
   hierarchy of needs   19, 19
negative emphasis   21, 21–22
Skinner, B F
   operant conditioning   20
social reinforcement   20–21, 113–14
Stajkovic, Alex and Luthans, Fred
   behaviourism   20
see also engagement

National Health Service (NHS)   120
national insurance on non-cash
      awards   93–98
   at the Department for Business,
      Innovation and Skills (BIS)   136
   at Edexcel   147
   exemptions
      for long service awards   97
      for suggestion schemes   96–97
   PAYE settlement agreements
      (PSAs)   95–96
   settlement by employer   93
National Lottery   121
national recognition awards
   armed forces   28–29
   national honours system   27–28
nationality, effect of   46–47
negative emphasis   21, 21–22
Nelson, Bob   63
non-cash awards   1
   choosing the award   58–62
      awards for the family   59
      and fun   61
      and highly-paid employees   61–62
      ideas for awards   59–60
      usual awards   60–61
   definition   2
   desirability of   115
   travel   115–16
   why it works   7–13, 112
      differentiation from pay   8–9
      Jeffrey research   7–8
      key jobs   13
      memory value   9–10, 10
      perceived value   11
      thought involved   11–12

O.C. Tanner Company, The   89
One Minute Manager, The   43

Order of the British Empire   29
Oscars@3   see 3

Pavlov, Ivan   20
PAYE settlement agreements (PSAs)
      95–96
Pearson plc   145
peers, recognition by   53
perceived value   11
Performance Enhancement Group   45
performance management
   at the annual review   102–04
   promotions   104
Pink, Dan   111
Platinum club   see RSA
Prince, The   16
Prudential
   case study   167–72
      award approval   170–71
      behaviours   167–68
      business overview   167
      manager guidance   168
      nominations   169
      performance management
         system   172
      'Recognition'   76, 168
      scheme reviews   171–72
      use of data   172
   and guidelines   33
   and local programmes   74
   and monitoring programme usage   71
   and team awards   46
   and third-party providers   79
   and values   34, 104

recognition
   definition of   1, 15–16
   and employee development   104–06,
      105
      role of line managers   106
   historical thinking on   16–17
   and incentives   31–32, 32
   at individual level   46
   key jobs   41
   and nationality   46–47
   in organizations   24–26
   at organizational level   44–46
   and performance management
      at the annual review   102–04
      promotions   104
   and reward
      incentive programmes   101–02
      relationship between recognition
         and reward   100
      reward as a motivator   101
   at team level   46

what to recognize
  cultural fit   37
  customer service   34
  failure   5
  using guidelines   32–33
  health and safety   35–36
  internal customer service   35
  long service   36–37
  management skills   36
  suggestions   38–39
  using values   33–34
when to recognize   38–41
  frequencies for reinforcement   39
  immediate recognition   39–40
  long-term recognition
    programmes   40–41
where it fits   104–05, 105
who should recognize   47–48
'Recognition'   see Prudential
recognition continuum   43
  day-to-day recognition   44
  formal recognition   44
  informal recognition   44
recognition programmes   40–41
  awards ceremonies   54–57
    as a celebration   54–55
    at Great Ormond Street Hospital
      (GOSH)   56
    at Haringey Council   56–57
    at the Metropolitan Police   55–56
  cost of
    average amount budgeted   90,
      90–91
    central vs local budgets   91–92
    finding the money   92
    what to budget for
  designing a programme
    adding new programmes   77–78,
      78
    and customer satisfaction
      surveys   71–73
    and defining objectives   68,
      68–69, 69
    and existing practices   74
    formal programmes   76–77
    and gradual improvement   73
    informal programmes   77
    key jobs   84
    and measuring outcomes   73
    naming the programme   76
    and personalization   69–70
    and programme usage   70
    and publicity   75
    and type of programme   73–74
  measuring the effectiveness of
    anecdotal evidence   85–86

    comparing results   87, 87
    effect on employee relations   88
    success stories   89, 89–90
    ways to measure   86–87, 86, 87
  prevalence of   2–5, 3
  and the public sector   4
  reviewing the programme   83–85
  using third-party providers   78–83
    advantages of   81
    and cost   80–81
    desirable qualities in   81–83
    types of provider   79–80
  use of, compared with cash   4, 4
Red Letter day   161
reward
  relationship between recognition and
    reward   100
  reward as a motivator   101
  see also incentive plans   101–02
Roffey Park Management Institute
    Survey   25
Round of applause   see 3
Royal Mail
  absenteeism   120
RSA   36, 71–73
  employee recognition shop   72
  Platinum club   72
  recognition score   72

Sainsbury's   169
Sears Roebuck   23
seasonal gifts   94
Skinner, B F 39
  operant conditioning   20
Sky   see British Sky Broadcasting Group
    plc
Skype   130
small gifts   94
Southwest Airlines   52, 54–55
Stajkovic, Alex and Luthans, Fred   20
Standard Chartered Bank plc
  case study   180–83
    annual performance appraisal   181
    business overview   180
    core values   180
    engagement survey   181–82
    local recognition programmes   183
    manager skills and role   182–83
  and day-to-day recognition   44
  and employee engagement   23, 47
  and line managers   48
  and local programmes   74
  and management training   106
  and performance rating   103
  and supporting managers   50
  and values   34

Star awards   *see* Edexcel
State of Human Resources Survey   24
Stephenson, Sir Paul   37
Sunday Times 100 Best Companies to
       Work For   3
Sunday Times Best Big Companies to Work
       For list   166

taxation on non-cash awards   93–98
    at the Department for Business,
           Innovation and Skills (BIS)   136
    at Edexcel   147
    exemptions
         for long service awards   36, 97
         for suggestion schemes   38,
           96–97
    key jobs
    PAYE settlement agreements
           (PSAs)   95–96
    settlement by employer   93
    taxed award schemes (TASs)   95–96
    'trivial' benefits   94–95
taxed award schemes (TASs)   95–96
team performance health check
           (TPHC)   *see* 3
third-party providers, using   78–83
    advantages of   81
    and cost   80–81
    desirable qualities in   81–83
    types of provider   79–80
Thorndike, Edward   20
Tiffany   131

Timpson, John   12, *12*
'trivial' benefits   94–95
'trophy value'   9
Tulgan, Bruce   45
Twitter   129
Tyson, Shaun   101

US Department of Labor   26

Victoria Cross   28
Vroom, Victor   112, 115

Wagner, Rod and Harter, James   67
Waitrose   163
Watson, John B   20
winners, creating   62–65
    and achievement   63–64
    and draws   64
    and implementing more than one
           programme   64–65
    and language   64
    and quotas   62
    and role models   63
*Working Life: Employee Attitudes and
       Engagement*   26
Workspan   10
World at Work 2008 survey   2, 60, 68, 86
WOW! Awards *see* Haringey Council

YouGov   23, 26
       People Index   23–24